No end of a lesson

The story of Suez

No end of a lesson

The story of Suez

Anthony Nutting

CONSTABLE LONDON

First published in Great Britain 1967
by Constable and Company Ltd
3 The Lanchesters, 162 Fulham Palace Road
London W6 9ER
Paperback edition 1996
Copyright © 1967 Anthony Nutting
ISBN 0 09 476820 X
Printed in Great Britain by
St Edmundsbury Press Ltd
Bury St Edmunds, Suffolk

A CIP catalogue record for this book
is available from the British Library

To Musa Alami of Jericho
in everlasting admiration of his
courage and compassion

Contents

Introduction to the New Edition

Forty years ago the British government engaged in a sordid conspiracy in collusion with France and Israel with the objective of toppling Egypt's current ruler, President Gamal Abdel Nasser, and repossessing the Suez Canal Company, which Nasser has nationalised three months earlier. With virtually the whole world against them—including the United States, the Soviet bloc and the Arab world—the conspirators were forced ignominiously to withdraw the forces they had sent to seize the Suez Canal and to accept that henceforth this vital waterway would be managed by an Egyptian administration.

As the only Minister privy to all the secrets of this insane adventure who opposed it from the outset, it fell to me to tell the story eleven years later, when all the principal British protagonists were out of office and when the revelation of their duplicity could therefore do no damage to the government of the day. Entitled *No End of a Lesson*, after the Kipling poem about the Boer War, my account was as much a cautionary tale as a confession of British wrong-doing, written at least partly in the hope that Britain would learn the lesson of Suez and shape her dealings with the Middle East accordingly. However, forty years on from this tragic episode, that hope remains unfulfilled.

As I warned Anthony Eden and Selwyn Lloyd in the run-up to Suez, for Britain and France to use Israel as their stalking-horse to attack Egypt was bound to confirm every Arab's suspicion that we had established the Israeli State not as a refuge for persecuted Jewry but as a beachhead from which to exercise our continued dominance over the Arab world. It therefore came as no surprise when, two years later, as a direct consequence of the Suez *débâcle*, Britain's most faithful Arab ally–the regime of Nuri Said in Iraq— was swept away in a bloody revolution. The Baghdad Pact, created by Eden and Nuri three years before, collapsed and with it all that remained of traditional British policy in the region.

Shortly thereafter Britain turned her back on the Middle East. British garrisons were withdrawn from the entire region. Paternalism turned into abdication and Britain handed over the torch to the Americans, no longer willing or able to impose the tutelage she had exercised for a hundred years over her erstwhile Arab protégés. True, she made a brief re-entry into the region to help evict Saddam Hussein from Kuwait in 1990. But for the rest she left it to the Americans to assume the mantle of Western leadership, refusing to acknowledge any responsibility for the legacy of her former misdeeds.

To understand the reasons for this act of abdication we have to remember that, from the middle of the nineteenth century up to the 1950s, British policy in the Middle East had been dominated by a concern, amounting at times to an obsession, over the security of the Suez Canal, the life-line of her eastern empire and, following World War I, of her oil supplies. Indeed, even before the Canal was dug, the threat posed by Napoleon's invasion of Egypt to her imperial communications with India had set Britain on a course that was to lead to her assertion of paramountcy in the region. British naval and military forces were despatched to evict the invaders and for all the rest of the nineteenth century British statesmen leaned over backwards to exclude foreign and, in particular, French influence from Egypt or, where this was not possible, to neutralise it.

When Ferdinand de Lesseps, backed by French finance, conceived the idea of digging the Suez Canal, Lord Palmerston used every available device and intrigue with the Ottoman Sultan—

Egypt's titular sovereign—to prevent what he saw as a devilish French threat to British influence and British imperial communications. These efforts failed and the Suez Canal Company was established as a Franco-Egyptian partnership in 1858. But when, eighteen years later, the Egyptian Khedive Ismail overspent himself into bankruptcy, Britain lost no time in reasserting her ascendancy by helping herself to his 44 per cent shareholding in settlement of his country's debts.

As part of the deal Britain also insisted on imposing a system of control over all future Egyptian revenue and expenditure to be exercised by British and French officials. Three years later Ismail sought to free himself from this arbitrary interference. But to no avail: Britain merely prevailed upon the Sultan to depose him in favour of his son. And when, in 1882, the Egyptian army rose in rebellion against this alien domination, British forces moved in effectively to occupy the country for what turned out to be the next seventy-three years.

However, by the end of the nineteenth century, Britain was no longer content to rely on control of Egypt alone to protect the Canal. The perceived threat to the Nile Valley of the Mahdi's rebellion in the Sudan, coupled with attempts by France to establish a belt of French dominion from West Africa to the Red Sea, led to the invasion of the Sudan in 1898. Brushing aside a token French force sent to thwart their advance, British forces defeated the rebels at Omdurman and proclaimed an Anglo-Egyptian Condominium—which system of government made the Sudan a virtual British colony for the next fifty-eight years. This further advance led to the occupation of Uganda to protect the Sudan and to the colonisation of Kenya as the supply route for Uganda.

Finally, after World War I, following the collapse of the Ottoman Empire and acting on the advice of Lord Kitchener during his period as de facto Viceroy of Egypt, Britain grabbed the mandates over Palestine and Transjordan. Never mind that she had pledged to the Arabs who had fought with her to defeat the Turks that these territories would enjoy independence after victory was achieved: Britain believed that she needed them to establish a forward base to ensure that the Canal would be defended in depth on both sides. So under the humanitarian cloak of the Balfour Declaration's offer of a Jewish national home in Palestine, the final link was forged in the chain of protection for the Canal.

Britain had thus been drawn into the scramble for Africa and the Middle East almost entirely by her obsessive concern for this imperial life-line. And even after India and most of the eastern empire had achieved independence, following the end of World War II, any apparent threat to the status quo of the Canal continued to bring an immediate knee-jerk reaction from Whitehall and Westminster. For oil had replaced India at the top of the list of British preoccupations overseas and the Canal was essential to the safe and speedy transport of this precious lubricant of British industry. Hence the reluctance of successive British governments to withdraw from their bases in Egypt, Iraq and Jordan after World War II in the face of a rising tide of opposition from Arab nationalism. And hence of course the near hysterical reaction of Eden's government to Nasser's nationalisation of the Suez Canal Company in 1956 following the withdrawal of the Anglo-American offer to help build the Aswan High Dam.

In fact, Nasser's action, vengeful and precipitate though it was, posed little more of a real threat to British interests than the nationalisation of the Anglo-Iranian Oil Company five years before—an issue which Eden, as Churchill's Foreign Secretary, had been happy to resolve by diplomatic negotiations with the Iranians. Yet the nationalisation of the Canal Company was treated as a virtual declaration of war in London. At best it was felt that, under Egyptian control, traffic through the Canal would come to a grinding halt, *The Times* newspaper remarking with a sneer that so complex and vital an international waterway could not be run 'by a nation with so low technical and managerial skills as the Egyptians'. At worst it was said that Nasser would out of spite discriminate against British shipping, although clearly it was now more than ever in Egypt's interest to increase traffic through the Canal to the maximum.

Nasser became Public Enemy No. I in England and also in

France where he was held to be mainly responsible for sustaining the resistance to French rule of the nationalist rebels in Algeria. From then on it was merely a matter of time before a pretext would be manufactured for waging war against Egypt and toppling Nasser from his perch.

In *No End of a Lesson* I have shown how the conspiracy which created this pretext was concocted and how, when the dust of the ensuing conflict settled, Britain, France and Israel were forced to beat an inglorious retreat. Far from being toppled, Nasser was more firmly entrenched than ever and Britain had found that she no longer had the power to wage war independently of her allies and in defiance of world opinion.

Most significant of all, the Egyptians were able to show that, mainly with Egyptian pilots, they could run the waterway just as effectively as the former company. For ten years later in 1966 no less than 274 million tons of shipping—well over double the pre-nationalisation figure—passed through the Canal. British ships suffered no difficulties or discrimination. Britain's precious oil supplies were as safe as ever.

After a century of obsessive fussing and fretting over the security of this 'life-line', Britain could now relax her vigil. The Suez Canal could look after itself and there was no longer a need to station British forces in the region to protect British interests. Indeed, as the revolution in Iraq and the mounting pressures of Arab nationalism elsewhere in the Arabian peninsula were to show, the very presence of British military bases was more likely to damage than to protect those interests. And so, by the early 'seventies, Britain had withdrawn from Jordan, Aden, Libya and the Gulf. The Arab world was free of British tutelage and Britain in her turn regarded herself as free of all further responsbility for the Middle East.

Meanwhile the Americans and, to a lesser extent, the Russians had moved in and the Middle East became a front line area of the Cold War. America supported Israel in her every action against the Arabs and, in particular, the Palestinians from the Six Days War in 1967 to the invasion of Lebanon in 1982 and aided and abetted her other ally, the Shah of Iran, in his fatal plunge into confrontation with the might of militant Islam. Russia responded, albeit somewhat half-heartedly, with military aid to Egypt and Syria in what proved to be a vain attempt to woo the forces of Arab nationalism. Meanwhile Britain adopted the role of onlooker, content to support her American allies no matter how biased their dealings might be. Successive British governments denied any further liability for the region's problems and insisted that it was a matter for the Super-Powers and in particular the United States to broker any peace settlement. So when President Carter pressured Anwar Sadat into accepting the Camp David agreement with Israel's Menachem Begin, which in effect merely neutralised Egypt at the expense of the Palestinians, Britain acclaimed the achievement without apparent reservations.

Today, thanks to Norwegian mediation, Israel and the Palestinians have taken the first faltering steps in a dialogue for a possible peace. But such is the depth of mutual hatred and suspicion engendered by seventy years of conflict that progress will inevitably be slow and fitful. And for this dialogue to bring about an eventual settlement a lot of outside pressure on both sides will be needed.

Such an even-handed role is clearly beyond the capacity of the Americans to fulfil. Dare one hope therefore that at long last Britain might step into the breach? For, however much British governments may seek to deny it, the fact remains that Britain does have a moral responsibility for the instability and dissension that have plagued the region ever since the end of World War I and of course a particular liability for the plight of the Palestinians.

Alone, Britain clearly does not have the diplomatic clout to bring about an Arab-Israeli deal. But with her European partners she could do much to influence the course of events in favour of justice and peace. If only to expunge the folly and iniquity of Suez, she owes it to herself to try.

17.6.96.

Preface

"Let us admit it fairly as a business people should.
We have had no end of a lesson, it will do us no end of
good."

Rudyard Kipling's well-known lines on the Boer War could
apply equally appropriately to the Suez disaster of 1956. The
Boer War, like the American War of Independence nearly 150
years before, showed that the Dutch colonists were not
prepared to submit to British imperialism: the Suez War, 50
years later, showed that Britain could no longer dictate to
Egypt.

Within the span of that turbulent half-century the world was
transformed and the conditions in which Britain had been able
to play her former imperial role ceased to exist. British rule
was withdrawn from vast areas of the world as the nineteenth-
century concept of Empire was swept away in the scalding
torrents of twentieth-century nationalism. Tel el-Kebir,
Omdurman and the Khyber Pass now belong in the history
books: the Wolseleys and the Kitcheners have ceased to be the
arbiters of the fate of nations which, regardless of size and
strength, now enjoy equality of status with the mightiest of
powers in the United Nations. And the lesson of the decline in
Britain's power to control events and dictate to governments which

started in South Africa at the turn of the century was to be completed in Egypt fifty years later.

It was my sad lot to witness from the inside this last dying convulsion of British imperialism and to see all my warnings against reverting to gunboat diplomacy ignored. Thus I was left with no alternative but to dissociate myself from the Government of the day by resigning my post as Minister of State for Foreign Affairs. Apart from a brief letter to the Prime Minister stating that I could not defend his policy any longer and must therefore ask him to accept my resignation, no explanation of my action has been vouchsafed by me until now. I made no statement to the House of Commons, although it is an almost invariable custom for a Minister who resigns on an issue of principle to do so, and, in all the newspaper acticles and books which I have written about Britain's relations with Egypt and the Arab world, I have avoided discussing the Suez *débâcle* in any but the most general terms.

The reasons for this long silence are very simple. Either I had to tell the whole story as I saw it, or say nothing at all. And so long as any of the chief protagonists of the Suez War still held high public office in Britain, it would have clearly been a grave disservice to the nation, which they still led and represented in the councils of the world, to have told the whole story. No doubt other nations and statesmen suspected that the Israeli attack on Egypt had been planned in collusion with Britain and France and that British Ministers at the time had sought to cover up their misdeeds by refusing to admit the truth. But to have publicly confirmed their suspicions would merely have made it impossible for them to have dealt with these same Ministers on a basis of confidence and trust.

Now, however, those who led us into this *débâcle* are out of office and, with one exception, out of politics, and Britain is represented by men who bear no responsibility for the decisions of ten years ago. The time has therefore come to reconsider whether the Suez story should be told in full or whether the veil of silence should be left undrawn. And I have decided to tell it, and to tell it now, for the following reasons.

First, I hope I may not be thought immodest in saying that I feel I owe it to history to tell it. Due to the intense security precautions taken at the time, only some half a dozen people in Britain today know the story as I know it—and of this 'select' group all but I myself were so involved in the venture that for them to reveal the truth now would involve an act of confession too mortifying for any man to volunteer. Added to this, since no records were kept, at least on the British side, of the discussions between Britain, France and Israel which led to the attack on Egypt, the historian will find no enlightenment in the archives of the Foreign Office when the official history of these times comes to be written. Thus it seems that I have a unique responsibility to set down in a simple, straightforward fashion the sequence of events of the Suez crisis. A number of books have been written since 1956 purporting to contain inside information culled from French and Israeli sources and offering a fuller and more dramatised account of these events than I have given. But in writing this memoir I have deliberately restricted myself to my own notes on what occurred and save where specifically stated, have only related that which I saw and heard with my own eyes and ears at the time.

Second, there have been over the past year or so several revelations by important participants in the Suez War, such as M. Christian Pineau, who was Foreign Minister of France at the time, and General Moshe Dayan, who commanded the Israeli army in the attack on Egypt. While not telling the whole story, these revelations have done enough to show that the explanations of Britain's part in the affair which were given to Parliament by British Ministers at the time were, to say the least, grossly misleading and disingenuous. What has not been explained is how and why Anthony Eden came to adopt a policy which was, at one and the same time, morally indefensible and politically suicidal. Thus, thanks to men such as Pineau and Dayan, the world now knows that Eden and his colleagues were parties to a sordid conspiracy with France and Israel to seize the Suez Canal; but little or nothing is known of the pressures, personal and public, physical and political, which drove Britain's twentieth-century Talleyrand to put upon himself the mantle of Napoleon. The purpose of this book, while in no sense an apologia any more than it is intended to be an indictment, is to fill this gap in public knowledge and to explain how and when and why Eden should have come to act so completely out of character.

Third, I have deliberately decided that it is only fair to publish this personal memoir in the lifetime of those who were involved. There is, of course, a school of thought which holds that books such as this should not appear until after the principal characters are dead. But I personally believe that, in this case at least, the participants should have the opportunity to speak for themselves and that it would be, in fact if not in intention, an act of cowardice to publish such a book after they are dead.

Finally, I have a personal reason for telling this strange and tragic story. The Suez episode and my resignation from the Government and from Parliament wrecked my political career. Much as I regret this and much as I hated having to give up a ministerial post of consuming interest, I have no complaints. If I had my life over again, I would have to do exactly as I did—although I suspect that if the clock could be put back to 1956 the need for me to do it would not arise a second time! Nevertheless, despite the revelations of Pineau and Dayan, there are still a number of people who cannot understand how I could have resigned from a Government led by the man who for so many years had been my political mentor. Although, as it turned out, my resignation was to damage nobody but myself, such people have been only too ready to join in the chorus of criticism led by certain newspapers both then and since and to accuse me of betraying my leader and patron. It is therefore perhaps pardonable, after a lapse of ten years and when the national interest is no longer at risk, that I should wish to answer these charges and to explain the stand which I took.

One of the disagreeable things about politics is that it sometimes requires that a choice be made between loyalty to principles and loyalty to friends. I was forced to make this choice and, while I chose to be loyal to principles, I can honestly say that I made my decision without any sense of bitterness towards the friends from whom I was to be parted. Likewise, in what I have written of the Suez War as I saw it, I have had no bitter feelings, only sadness that it should have fallen to my lot to participate in, and now to relate, this tragic chapter of England's history. Inevitably I have been highly critical in places of those whom I served, but I trust that they will do me the justice of confirming that such criticism is not the product of hindsight and that I was as adamant in opposing their policies at the time as I am now in reasserting that what they did was morally wrong and politically insane. If as a result my account should seem shocking or even offensive to some people, or to be a departure from 'convention', I make no apologies. For there is, as there can be, no convention which allows a government to deceive Parliament and people and, sheltering behind that deception, to lead the nation into war, yet which denies the right of one, who dissociated himself from that deception by resigning his office, to reveal the truth.

Cap Spartel,
Morocco.   September 1966.

I Metamorphosis of a Statesman

The drama that was to become the Suez disaster actually began on March 1, 1956. In the early afternoon of that day the Prime Minister of Jordan sent for the British Ambassador and told him that King Hussein had just given a personal order for the immediate dismissal of General Glubb from the post of Chief of the General Staff and Commander of the Arab Legion, Jordan's army. A few hours later, after the news had reached London, the Prime Minister of Great Britain declared a personal war on the man whom he held responsible for Glubb's dismissal—Gamal Abdel Nasser, President and Prime Minister of Egypt. For Eden, such a blow to Britain's waning prestige as an imperial power, capable of influencing men and events in the Middle East, could not be allowed to go unpunished. The summary sacking of this venerable British officer, who had served Jordan for twenty-five years and commanded the Arab Legion since 1939, was a challenge which no British Government, least of all a Conservative Government, could lightly dismiss. And the 'fact' that it had been engineered by an upstart dictator in Egypt made it all the more intolerable and hence imperative to stage some spectacular and crushing remonstrance against the instigator of Britain's humiliation.

Anthony Eden has since said in his memoir, *Full Circle,* that he is 'now convinced' that the King's attitude towards his

British Commander-in-Chief was partly inspired by 'jealousy of a younger man for an older one long established in a position of authority in the country'. But, as one who spent the evening and half of the night after Glubb's dismissal arguing with Eden, I can testify that, at the time, he put all the blame on Nasser and brushed aside every argument that more personal considerations had in fact influenced Hussein's arbitrary decision. And on that fatal day he decided that the world was not big enough to hold both him and Nasser. The 'Egyptian dictator' had to be eliminated somehow or other, else he would destroy Britain's position in the Middle East and Eden's position as Prime Minister of Britain.

How and why was this mortal decision arrived at? And how and why did the man, whose whole political career and reputation had been founded on his genius for negotiation, act so wildly out of character? How did Eden of all people come to play the decisive role in the sordid disaster of the Suez War?

For answers to these questions it is necessary first to go back several years. After the General Election of 1951, Eden returned to the Foreign Office, where a whole series of dangerous crises awaited him. In Iran Premier Mossadeq had nationalised the oil industry and the Anglo-Iranian Oil Company had been thrown out. In Egypt King Farouk's Ministers had denounced the 1936 Treaty with Britain which allowed the stationing of British forces in the Suez Canal Zone until 1956, a Treaty which Eden had himself signed during his first spell as Foreign Secretary. In Korea there was a full-scale war between North and South, with Chinese Communist 'volunteers' helping the North Koreans, while the South were supported by United Nations forces, made up for the most part of American units, supported by British and Commonwealth contingents. In Indo-China the French colonial régime was beginning to crumble before nationalist pressures, aided and abetted by Communist China. Italy and Yugoslavia were at loggerheads over their claims to the city of Trieste. And over all this unhappy scene the voices of the Great Powers were raised against each other in

violent argument and abuse. The Cold War was at its height.
The world was divided by a chasm of political and ideological
conflict and, symptomatic of that division, Germany and
Austria lay dismembered and occupied by their bitterly bicker-
ing conquerors with no sign of a peace treaty to ease the agony
of their six-year-old defeat.

Eden's first reaction to this daunting catalogue of crises was
typical. In a speech at the U.N. General Assembly he called
for an end to abuse and accusation and invited his fellow delegates from all countries to join him in grasping 'definite and
limited problems and working for their practical solution'. And
he concluded by saying, 'That is the real road to peace. That
is the way to make a fresh start.' What is more, that is precisely
what he did during the next three and a half years that he remained Foreign Secretary. And when he took over the Premiership from Sir Winston Churchill in April, 1955, no man could
claim a prouder record of international settlements than
Anthony Eden. He had negotiated a settlement of the Iranian
oil dispute, and British oil men were back in Abadan. Agreement had been reached with Egypt for the withdrawal of British
forces and for the operation by British civilian contractors of a
servicing base in the Canal Zone for British military equipment, which was to be run in partnership with the Egyptian
armed forces. In Korea, after months of deadlocked negotiations for an armistice, he and Selwyn Lloyd, then Minister of
State in the Foreign Office, had been instrumental in cutting
the Gordian knot and bringing about a settlement. In Indo-
China, against the extreme reluctance of the French to admit
defeat and the equally extreme desire of the Americans to use
Indo-China as a demonstration area to warn Communist China
about America's superior strength, he performed the almost
superhuman task of persuading all parties, including the
Chinese, to agree to a settlement. Likewise Italy and Yugoslavia had been induced to make up their quarrel over Trieste.
And while no agreement had been possible for the reunifica-
tion of Germany, because of Russian objections, the equivalent

of a peace treaty had been signed with West Germany, who had become a respected partner of the western community as a member of N.A.T.O. Finally, although the Cold War was not over yet, the Great Powers had at least met at the conference table on a number of occasions and, in Churchill's memorable phrase, 'jaw-jaw' had replaced 'war-war'. Disarmament talks had been started between Russia, America, France and ourselves. And, to round off the list of successes, in the middle of the General Election of 1955, the Russians finally relented in their opposition to Austrian independence and, together with Britain, France and the United States, signed a peace treaty with Austria on May 15.

Eden could be justly proud of this record, which was owed so largely to his dogged determination and real skill as a negotiator. And it needed only the subtle reminder to the electorate of a national poster campaign depicting his photograph with the words, 'Working for Peace', as a caption, to secure him a comfortably increased majority in the election, one of the very few in modern history to be fought and won largely on foreign, as distinct from domestic, issues. The first Summit Conference of the leaders of Russia, America, Britain and France was to be held a few weeks later in July; and to the majority of the voters it seemed inconceivable that Britain should be represented at such a crucial meeting by anyone but the man who had brought settlement and peace in so many areas where hitherto there had been only dispute and war.

For a while after his General Election triumph, I detected no change in Eden's attitude to foreign affairs which could not be explained by the removal of his former close association with the Foreign Office which his departure to No. 10, Downing Street, inevitably entailed. He allowed the new Foreign Secretary, Harold Macmillan, considerable latitude and there was no suggestion of that constant interference in matters of detail which he was later to visit upon Selwyn Lloyd when he took over from Macmillan. Apart from the Summit Conference, which ended as expected in an agreement to differ on all major issues, he was more concerned in those first few months with domestic problems, such as the railway strike. If anything, where foreign affairs were concerned, he seemed readier than ever to try conciliation. He invited the Russian leaders, Marshal Bulganin and Mr. Khrushchev, to visit London for talks in the following April. When I sought his authority to launch a new initiative in the disarmament talks with the Russians, he was all for it. And even over Cyprus, an issue which as Foreign Secretary he had refused point-blank to discuss with the Greeks, for whom he had a strangely bitter dislike and distrust, he was now ready to try for a negotiated settlement. No longer did he contend that, as a British colony, Cyprus was 'undiscussable' with any foreign power; and he willingly allowed Macmillan to call a conference with Greek and Turkish representatives to try to work out a solution acceptable to the Greek and Turkish communities in the island.

Even when Egypt announced in September, 1955, that, having failed to obtain the arms she had expected from Britain after the signature of the 1954 agreement, she was to purchase equipment from the Soviet bloc countries, Eden did not react violently. Up to this point his attitude towards Egypt had been fairly open. He did not like Nasser personally, though he regarded him as a great improvement on King Farouk, and at their only meeting—which took place in the previous February when Eden was on his way to a conference in the Far East—he had greeted the Egyptian President with the utmost coldness. But a few months before this, after I had concluded the negotiations for the 1954 agreement about our bases, he had instructed me to stay on in Cairo and try to get on terms with Nasser and draw him out on the possibilities of future Anglo-Egyptian co-operation.

Eden had been justifiably disappointed that, so soon after we had supposedly removed the last irritant in our relations with Egypt—the presence of British troops in the Canal Zone —Nasser should have not only failed to bury the hatchet, but actually launched a violent radio attack on Nuri es-Said,

Britain's oldest Arab ally, for joining with Britain and Turkey
in the Baghdad Pact alliance, concluded early in 1955. But
while Eden might resent Nasser's attacks on our friends in the
Middle East, he was at heart friendly towards the Arab world.
And although he naturally shared the universal horror of all
civilised people over the sufferings of the Jewish people at the
hands of Nazi Germany, his sympathies in the Arab-Israel conflict had hitherto lain with the Arabs, who had lost their land
in face of Zionist incursions. He was appalled at the injustice
done to hundreds of thousands of Arab refugees from Palestine, who had been evicted from their homes to make room for
Jewish immigrants. And in his first Guildhall speech as Prime
Minister, he had spoken of the need for compromise over
Israel's frontiers as an essential precondition of any peace
settlement agreeable to the Arabs. He fully understood how
every Arab state, out of a feeling of brotherhood with the dis-
possessed Arabs of Palestine, should have retaliated with an
economic boycott of Israel. And, as I recall from a conversation
which we had in Berlin in January, 1954, he had then
held most emphatically that, as an Arab country still in a state
of war with Israel, Egypt had an arguable claim—under
Article 10 of the Constantinople Convention governing the
Suez Canal—to deny passage to Israeli ships as a measure
necessary to 'assure ... the defence of Egypt'. Selwyn Lloyd
had, in Eden's absence, written a minute to the Prime Minister
denying that Egypt had any such right and, on learning of this,
Eden had waxed very angry and hastened to correct his Minister of State.

His views had not, of course, been shared by Churchill,
whose strong sympathies lay with the Zionist cause. Still less
were they acceptable to certain newspapers, notably the *Daily
Telegraph* and the *Daily Express,* and to a section of opinion
in the Conservative Party known as the Suez Group, a hotch-
potch collection of embittered ex-Ministers and young newly
elected back-benchers anxious to cut a figure in Parliament by
attacking the Government for selling out British imperial in-

terests. The Suez Group had bitterly opposed the withdrawal of British troops from the Canal Zone. Ignoring the need for redeployment of our strength in the Middle East in places where British troops were less unwelcome than in Egypt, and brushing aside the fact that our forces would have to leave the Canal Zone anyway in 1956, when the 1936 Treaty came to an end, they denounced our evacuation as another 'scuttle' and a humiliating lowering of the flag.

Yet such was Eden's ascendancy in the Conservative Party after his impressive run of international settlements that he had been able to fend off all the attacks of the critics and to do the deal with Egypt which logic and Britain's strategic interests demanded. And, after his electoral triumph as Prime Minister, notwithstanding the Egyptian arms purchase from the Soviet bloc, when the question of a loan to Egypt to build the Aswan High Dam came up for discussion in 1955, he willingly joined with the United States in pledging a British contribution. The alternative, he felt, was to let Egypt turn to Russia, as she had already done for arms. 'And,' he told me, 'on no account must we let the Russians into the Nile Valley.'

But while Eden was able to conduct his foreign policy free from any serious challenge from Press or parliament, trouble was brewing for him on the home front as soon as he started his Premiership. The spectre of inflation had reappeared and our balance of payments had begun to tip dangerously. Wage increases, coupled with tax reductions, were pushing prices up as the nation enjoyed a new spending spree. A tightening of the 'credit squeeze' in July had failed to halt the inflationary spiral and to bridge the gap between exports and imports; our gold and dollar reserves were being run down at the rate of $100 million a month. By September it became clear that some drastic action must be taken to curb inflation and that such action involved the introduction of a supplementary Budget.

On October 26 the Chancellor of the Exchequer, Rab Butler, presented his proposals to the House of Commons. These involved considerable curbs on Government and private spend-

ing, a reduction in the manpower of the armed forces to swell
the ranks of civilian labour, a postponement of long-term in-
vestment plans for the electricity and gas industries and the
railways, a reduction in the housing programme and an increase
in purchase tax and taxation of distributed profits. Inevitably
the Labour Opposition, led by Hugh Gaitskell, himself a former Chancellor of the Exchequer, denounced the Government
for having played fast and loose with the nation's economy for
political gain. The April Budget, which contained none of these
cuts and curbs, had been framed to buy the electors' votes,
Gaitskell claimed, despite the fact that inflation was already rife
at that time. The Government had won the election with their
false financial prospectus, with the result that inflation had got
out of control, and they had now come to Parliament with the
very measures that they should have had the courage and
honesty to impose before the election.

It was a formidable argument, and although Butler made a
masterly reply to the accusations levelled at him, his days as
Chancellor of the Exchequer were clearly numbered. A few
weeks after he had finished piloting his supplementary Budget
through the House of Commons, Eden announced a major reshuffle of the Government. Butler became Lord Privy Seal and
the Leader of the House of Commons. Macmillan took over
the Treasury and Selwyn Lloyd, whom I had succeeded as
Minister of State in the Foreign Office, left the Ministry of
Defence to take Macmillan's place as Foreign Secretary.

The reshuffle let Butler out of a tight corner and, as some
thought, an untenable position. But it did not let out Eden,
who as Prime Minister was held ultimately responsible for the
'stop-go' policy which had brought about the supplementary
Budget. A feeling began to grow that, after three years of steady
economic expansion, we were drifting back to the recurrent
cycle of crises which had haunted us throughout the immediate
post-war period. And with this feeling criticism mounted
against Eden personally. He had lost his grip on events, it was
said. His inexperience of financial and economic problems was

beginning to show. The deft diplomat was no leader; he had no control over his Ministers. Inevitably comparisons were drawn between him and his predecessor and he was seen to be dwarfed by the mantle of Churchill. Rab Butler, in an effort to defend his leader, added fuel to the critics' fire with the curiously back-handed compliment that Eden was 'the best Prime Minister we've got'. But of all the attacks which fell upon him the one which hurt the most came from an editorial in the *Daily Telegraph* accusing the Prime Minister of weakness. Describing how, when addressing a public meeting, Eden would frequently seek to emphasise a point by placing the clenched fist of one hand in the open palm of the other, the *Telegraph* commented, 'but the smack is seldom heard'!

This smack was heard and felt in Downing Street, however. I had never seen Eden so stricken. He was positively writhing in the agony of this barbed shaft which, unlike some of the blunter and cruder assaults of the Opposition, had struck him at his weakest point. He was not a leader in the Churchill tradition and nothing could ever make him so. He was a negotiator, a mediator *par excellence*. He was not a strategist who set a course for five, ten or twenty years ahead and stuck to it with bulldog determination. He was essentially a tactician who planned his advance in limited moves, stopping and starting, veering and tacking according to the strength and direction of the prevailing pressures. All of which had its advantages in dealing with foreign affairs, but when applied to home policies spelled 'stop-go' and hence vacillation. And here was a Conservative newspaper telling him to stop vacillating—in effect, to change his very character.

Eden resolved to strike back at his critics. Shortly after the *Telegraph* editorial appeared, he was due to make an important speech at Bradford, and he decided to use this occasion for his counter-attack. When he told me of his decision and showed me the form of words which he was going to use, I begged him to ignore the critics. We were going through a bad patch, but this was the inevitable result of having timed the General

Election exactly right. Had he waited until the autumn to ask for a new mandate from the electorate, he might have got a very different result. But things would improve and, with a comfortable majority in Parliament, he could afford to sit tight and wait for the improvement, when he would be able to throw the critics' words back in their teeth.

It was no good. For my pains I was told that I knew nothing about politics and that I had the mentality of a mere Foreign Office official! Eden went ahead and made his speech in Bradford, where naturally his digs at the London newspapers were wildly cheered by his provincial audience. But in London the delighted critics cried, '*Touché*'; and the campaign against him gathered increasing momentum. It was a difficult situation for the toughest politician. But Eden was not tough; he had not been hardened by criticism. For too long he had been the 'Golden Boy' of the Conservative Party, the man who resigned over Neville Chamberlain's appeasement policy and was proved right within less than two years, the 'Crown Prince' who basked in the sunshine of Churchill's admiration. And the storm which had struck him so suddenly and so soon after realising his life's ambition to become Prime Minister hurt his pride and shook his self-confidence.

It did something else too. The nervous tension which it stirred up inside him began to react on his constitution. In 1953, when undergoing an operation to remove his gall-bladder, he had suffered grave damage to his bile-duct, the 'exhaust-pipe' of the human system. A famous American surgeon had patched him up, but the patchwork was liable to wear out under extreme nervous pressure. And from now on the nervous pressures and tensions were to grow greater almost week by week, as the winter of the critics' discontent wore on.

There was, however, one consolation, at least until the Glubb episode. Whatever the problems at home, on the international front all seemed quiet and well. True, there had been no more spectacular settlements and the meeting of the Great Powers' Foreign Ministers following the summer Summit Conference had ended in a stalemate. But a visit to Washington in January, 1956, had revealed that America and Britain were officially at one on all major topics, including the Middle East. In particular Eden and President Eisenhower agreed that the Aswan Dam project should go forward with American and British aid and that, if Nasser showed willing to co-operate, the Western allies should reciprocate. In the Middle East we had suffered a reverse when a month earlier an attempt to induce Jordan to join the Baghdad Pact, with a promise to supply large quantities of tanks, guns and fighter aircraft, resulted in violent protests by the nationalists and had to be abandoned. There was some rioting in Amman, Jordan's capital; and Cairo Radio was quick to support the nationalist opposition, while Saudi Arabia, the traditional foe of the Hashemite Kings of Jordan and Iraq, made threatening gestures on Jordan's southern borders. But things had calmed down a lot since then and the situation had reverted to normal. And then on March 1 the blow fell.

General Glubb, after a lifetime of service to the Arab world, most of it spent in Jordan, had been dismissed at twenty-four hours' notice, together with his senior British officers. A bitter blow had been struck at British prestige. And for Eden, coming on top of all his domestic discomfitures, this was the last straw. Not only was he in trouble on the home front, but now, even in the international sphere, where he was the acknowledged expert, the dice seemed to be loaded against him. Bitterly, he now reproached himself for his previous Egyptian policy. This reverse, he insisted, was Nasser's doing. For months he had been hard at work trying to undermine General Glubb as a British officer commanding an Arab army and as the principal obstacle to his 'ambitions' to absorb Jordan. Nasser had prevented Jordan joining the Baghdad Pact, and now he had got rid of Glubb. Nasser was our Enemy No. 1 in the Middle East and he would not rest until he had destroyed all our friends and eliminated the last vestiges of our influence. If he succeeded, it would be the end of Eden. Nasser must therefore be himself destroyed.

2 Dismissal of General Glubb

To add insult to injury, Selwyn Lloyd, who was on his way to a conference in Karachi when Glubb was sacked, was greeted by a rioting mob during a brief stop-over in Bahrain, and his car was reported to have been stoned on the way from the airport to the British Residency. (In fact, his car was untouched, he later told me, and another car in the cortège containing members of his staff was spattered by a few handfuls of mud thrown by some anti-British rioters.) And when on top of this the nationalists in Jordan celebrated Glubb's dismissal with street demonstrations and anti-imperialist banners, Eden's reaction was almost as if No. 10 itself had been attacked and a howling mob of Arabs were laying siege to Downing Street.

His first instinct when the news of Hussein's decision reached him was to telegraph personally to the King to say that if he persisted in removing Glubb our relations with Jordan would be at an end. This would have meant no more British subsidy, no more British arms, the withdrawal of the force which we had moved to Jordan from the Canal Zone, and, of course, the removal of all remaining British officers from the Arab Legion. With the greatest difficulty I managed to dissuade him from making such a threat, on the grounds that it would force Hussein to turn to Egypt—the one thing Eden wished to avoid. To gain this point I had to concede that every British officer serving with the Jordan army should be ordered home.

However, although we argued far into the night of that fatal March 1, my arguments had no success in shaking Eden's absolute conviction that Glubb's dismissal was Nasser's doing. How else, he demanded, could we explain that the King had given not the slightest intimation, either on his frequent visits to London or in his regular meetings with our Ambassador in Amman, that he wanted to get rid of Glubb? Far from there having been any suggestion that Hussein disliked his general, relations between the two had been consistently cordial, and, only the day before he was sacked, Glubb had had a perfectly friendly talk with the King. Therefore the whole business reeked of Nasser's intrigues.

To make matters worse, Eden reminded us, the Foreign Secretary had passed through Cairo on his way to the Karachi conference, and he had seen Nasser, who was all smiles and smooth words. Yet at the very moment that Nasser was cooing like a dove to Lloyd, he was giving orders for the removal of General Glubb. I tried to suggest that, while Nasser might be delighted to see Glubb depart from Jordan, just as he had been to get rid of British troops from Egypt, a more probable explanation of Hussein's action was that he had decided that he could never be King in his own kingdom so long as Glubb was there with his infinitely greater experience and even prestige. It might be churlish to sack a man who had served the Hashemite throne for so many years at a mere day's notice. But 'tribal justice' was always swiftly executed and tribal traditions were deeply engrained in this desert kingdom.

In vain did I argue on these lines. Eden would have none of it. I could see no wrong in anything Nasser did, I was told, despite the fact that for months he had been trying to undermine every British interest and ally in the Middle East. 'You love Nasser,' he burst out, 'but I say he is our enemy and he shall be treated as such.' I retorted that I had always tried to avoid taking likes or dislikes for individual foreign leaders and I reminded Eden that it was he who had taught me this salutary rule, even though he did not always obey it himself. 'All I am trying to do,' I concluded, 'is to establish the true facts and to avoid attributing to Nasser victories which are not properly his.'

Within a few days I was able to prove much of what I had been saying to the Prime Minister. General Glubb came to see me at the Foreign Office on the morning after his return from Jordan. He was superbly unresentful over his abrupt dismissal, but still dazed by the speed of events during the past forty-eight hours and unable to account for the King's action. His relations with Hussein had never been better, he insisted. But when I pressed him to say if there had ever been disagreements for instance, about appointments in the Army, he said, 'Oh! yes. I often had to stop the King doing silly things, like promoting people who I knew were dishonest or incompetent. But after all, I was responsible as the Army's commander.' When I pointed out that this kind of attitude, that the King was 'interfering' in his own army, however justified on military grounds, might have turned Hussein against him, Glubb thought for a full minute and then, with that engaging, soft smile of his, he said, 'Yes. Perhaps you're right.' Then he left to go to Chequers, where I hoped he would be given an opportunity to say the same thing to Eden.

The day before Glubb came to see me I had another visitor whose knowledge of Jordan and of the Hashemite family was second to none—Sir Alexander Kirkbride, who had fought with T. E. Lawrence and had spent all but the last four years of his career in Palestine or Transjordan, working with Hussein's grandfather, King Abdullah, and finishing up as Ambassador to Jordan from 1946 to 1951. He was now on his way, in a purely private capacity, to open an archaeological museum in Jerusalem, and he wished to know if the Foreign Office felt he should still go and, if so, whether there was anything he could do to throw any light on the troubled situation. Jumping at the opportunity to get this expert 'second opinion' on what had prompted Hussein, I told him that we should be delighted if he went to Jordan and succeeded in drawing out the King, who had been somewhat uncommunicative in explaining himself to our Ambassador.

Kirkbride duly went, and on his arrival in Amman was overwhelmed with greetings. In the town he met a demonstration with banners and slogans, proclaiming 'Death to the Imperialists' and 'Down with British interference'. He had not gone more than a few yards when he was recognised and a crowd surrounded him, calling him their long-lost friend and bidding him welcome back to Jordan. It must have been an incongruous sight, with the towering Britisher who had spent most of his life running their affairs, surrounded by anti-Imperialist banners and being greeted by the leaders of the demonstration.

At the Royal Palace it was the same. The palace staff ran to shake his hand as he climbed the steps to the entrance. And inside, the King, quite beside himself with joy and relief at seeing Kirkbride, poured out his heart to this lifelong friend of his family. As he talked, all his pent-up indignation against Glubb came tumbling out. He could not, he said, have tolerated the General for another day; he had been patronised for too long and he was sick and tired of it. He could never be master in his own house so long as Glubb commanded the Army; and once he had made up his mind to get rid of him what was the sense in delaying? For Glubb to have stayed under an extended period of notice would have been to invite trouble in the Army.

When Kirkbride returned home a few days later, he reported his findings to Eden. Since I was asked to attend as well, in Selwyn Lloyd's continued absence abroad, I had a unique opportunity to observe the effect of this first-hand account of Hussein's motives on Eden personally. He was clearly put out by what Kirkbride had to say. He would far rather have continued to believe that Glubb's dismissal was all Nasser's doing. But he had to respect Kirkbride's experience and his conclusion that the King had told him the truth. Still, whatever the facts might be, the appearances were that Nasser, with his frequent radio attacks on Britain's allies in the Arab world, was at the bottom of it all. Certainly the Suez Group of Conservative M.P.s were taking this line and blaming this blow to our prestige on the 'scuttle' from our Canal Zone base. If we had stood firm against Nasser, instead of giving way to him, they argued, Glubb would still be Commander of the Arab Legion. And while Eden now realised that Hussein had acted on his own initiative, he was not prepared to argue this delicate point with the Suez Group. Besides, even if Nasser were not responsible for Glubb's removal, he would not rest until he had done Britain some other injury, perhaps more critical still. Therefore the declaration of war stood and Eden only awaited a pretext to put it into effect.

From now on Eden completely lost his touch. Gone was his old uncanny sense of timing, his deft feel for negotiation. Driven by the impulses of pride and prestige and nagged by mounting sickness, he began to behave like an enraged elephant charging senselessly at invisible and imaginary enemies in the international jungle. In the parliamentary debate on Glubb's dismissal, he made the worst speech of his whole career.

Admittedly it was an awkward debate, with the Government somewhat on the defensive, largely because Eden, instead of playing this unhappy episode down, had dramatised it into a *cause célèbre*. It was also one of those debates in which there was only one real speech to be made for the Government, which was the opening speech. I begged Eden to make it and to let me wind up, but he refused. He much preferred winding up, which gave him an opportunity to use his debating skills and, although I pointed out that he would have nothing to say except to reply to the jibes of the critics—scarcely a very dignified role for a Prime Minister—he insisted that I should open and he wind up.

His speech was a shambles. Inevitably he was left with nothing to say except a few debating points totally unworthy of a man in his position. As he carried on amid constant interruptions, I felt more and more embarrassed for him. And then, to the horrified amazement of his supporters, he finally lost his temper, something I had never seen him do before in all the eleven years that I had sat with him in the House of Commons. On the following day at a lunch party at No. 10 he tried to make a joke about how much worse his speech had been than mine. But as we discussed the debate and the situation that gave rise to it, a feeling came over me that I was talking to a total stranger. No longer did we see things in the same way; a wide gulf was now between us; and I knew then that nothing about our old relationship would ever be the same again. What I did not know was how much of this metamorphosis was due to sickness and to the poison from the damaged bile-duct, which was eating away at his whole system.

A few days later the extent of the change in Eden was further brought home to me. On the Monday after the Glubb debate I was playing host at a dinner at the Savoy Hotel given for Mr. Harold Stassen, my American colleague on the U.N. Disarmament Commission, who had come to London for a further round of discussions with the Russians in the five-power Disarmament Sub-committee. Earlier that day I had sent the Prime Minister a memorandum on the Middle East, suggesting one or two ways of strengthening our position in the area and of shedding unrewarding responsibilities. First, I had suggested that we should tell the United Nations that it was high time they took over the responsibility for keeping the peace between Israel and her Arab neighbours. Under the Tripartite Declaration of 1950, issued by America, France and ourselves, we three powers were alone responsible for preventing either side from starting another 'round' in the Arab-Israeli struggle, and there was every reason why this responsibility should be more widely shared. I had in mind a form of permanent U.N. police force stationed on Israel's borders. This would relieve us of the obligation—which could all too easily arise in the inflamed state of Arab-Israeli relations—of having to fight against an Arab state, such as Jordan, with whom we had a treaty of alliance. It would also enable us to reduce or

withdraw our forces in Jordan or elsewhere in the Middle East
if either political or military requirements demanded it.

My second suggestion was that we should step up our aid,
military and economic, to our friends in the Arab world. Bearing in mind how our refusal to deliver to Nasser the arms for
which he asked had sent him shopping in the Soviet bloc, I
felt that we should do all in our power to ensure that Iraq,
Jordan and the Persian Gulf sheikhdoms were built up with
British aid and British arms. Finally, realising that it would be
useless to oppose head-on Eden's declaration of war on
Nasser, I tried to soften and divert him with suggestions for
neutralising Nasser's attacks on our interests. This could be
done by, for instance, spelling out his Guildhall proposals for
concessions by Israel on frontiers, refugees and the Jordan
waters problems, as well as by helping Israel's Arab neighbours
to secure their defences. For by such words and deeds we
would be demonstrating to the Arab world that we wished to
see justice done for their cause.

To the Foreign Office advisers, who helped me to compose
this memorandum, all these suggestions seemed unexception-
able. Yet when they reached No. 10 later that evening, they
caused an explosion. In the middle of dinner with Stassen I
was called to the telephone. 'It's me,' said a voice which I recognised as the Prime Minister's. If his esoteric self-introduction
was meant to conceal his identity from the Savoy Hotel switch-
board, our subsequent conversation could hardly have done
more to defeat his purpose.

'What's all this poppycock you've sent me?' he shouted. 'I
don't agree with a single word of it.'

I replied that it was an attempt to look ahead and to ration-
alise our position in the Middle East, so as to avoid in the future
the kind of blow to our prestige that we had just suffered over
Glubb.

'But what's all this nonsense about isolating Nasser or
"neutralising" him, as you call it? I want him destroyed, can't
you understand? I want him removed, and if you and the

Foreign Office don't agree, then you'd better come to the Cabinet and explain why.'

I tried to calm him by saying that, before deciding to destroy Nasser, it might be wise to look for some alternative who would not be still more hostile to us. At the moment there did not appear to be any alternative, hostile or friendly. And the only result of removing Nasser would be anarchy in Egypt.

'But I don't want an alternative,' Eden shouted at me. 'And I don't give a damn if there's anarchy and chaos in Egypt.'

With this he hung up, leaving me to return to my dinner. I felt as if I had had a nightmare, only the nightmare was real.

Illusions of Imperialism

The immediate result of the Glubb episode was a toughening of British policy everywhere in the Middle East and the Eastern Mediterranean. And in the Cabinet it was the day of the 'whiff of grape-shot' school, represented by what one enlightened Minister called 'those overgrown Boy Scouts, personified by Duncan Sandys'. In those former appendages of the Indian Empire, the Persian Gulf sheikhdoms of Kuwait, Bahrain, Muscat and Oman, the smallest incident or affront to the British protecting power was treated as a major challenge, inspired, of course, by the arch-enemy, Nasser. A group of Bahraini merchants, who had formed themselves into a reformist society entitled the Committee of National Union, were branded as agitators executing Nasser's instructions to destroy all British influence in the Persian Gulf. In fact, all that these highly respectable and conservative practicians of private enterprise were seeking was a few constitutional reforms in a system of government so archaic and autocratic that it even denied to its subjects such means of understanding and communication as a newspaper.

When riots broke out in Bahrain following the Foreign Secretary's brief visit, Eden put the blame on the Committee of National Union. The 'whiff of grape-shot' school suggested that troops of the 'Strategic Reserve' be sent from Aden to quell the riots; and when the War Office pointed out that there were not enough troops to spare, Eden proposed to invite Nuri es-Said to help with the despatch of an Iraqi police detachment. In vain I argued that such action would only play into Nasser's hands and give him still more ammunition for his radio attacks on Britain and her 'imperialist stooges', such as Nuri. I was told that the Foreign Office evidently did not care a rap for British prestige, but that a Conservative Government was not going to allow Nasser and his agents to undermine us with impunity.

Fortunately, Eden's proposal came to nothing, because the Iraqi police authorities managed to persuade Nuri that their men would probably refuse to fire on their fellow Arabs and that their very presence in Bahrain, whether passive or active, might well spark a revolution in which Iraq would then be embroiled. A few days later quiet was restored in Bahrain, the Ruler conceded some of the demands of the reformists and the Committee of National Union accepted the compromise. But unfortunately this did not satisfy Eden. He wanted a demonstration of strength, an assertion of Britain's power and influence, to raise her battered prestige. Frustrated in the Persian Gulf, he decided to show the mailed fist in Cyprus.

At that particular moment the Governor of Cyprus, Sir John Harding, was in the throes of discussing the terms of a possible settlement of the island's future with Archbishop Makarios, the leader of the Greek Cypriot community. The tripartite conference between Britain, Greece and Turkey, which Macmillan had staged in the previous August, had ended in deadlock. The Greeks had insisted on self-determination for the island. But the Turks, concluding that, with a four-to-one majority of Greek Cypriots over Turkish, this would probably result in Cyprus opting for union with Greece, resolutely opposed self-determination. Britain, whose interests in the colony were almost entirely determined by her need for military and air bases which might be threatened by a union of Cyprus with Greece, supported the Turkish case. Having failed to get agreement internationally, the Government had in the early autumn sent Sir John Harding, an acknowledged military authority who had just relinquished the post of C.I.G.S., to try to reach a settlement with Makarios which would give Britain the security of tenure that she required for her bases.

The talks had been going on intermittently since October, but without result. Meanwhile, the terrorist attacks on British troops and installations by the Greek Cypriot resistance movement, E.O.K.A., which had started the trouble in this island, continued unabated and a State of Emergency had been declared. Whether or not Makarios was directly responsible for these acts of violence, his refusal to condemn them certainly acted as a spur to the perpetrators. And that he should have been discussing settlements with the Governor while British troops were being killed by terrorists naturally caused deep indignation within the Government at home. What is more, by March it appeared clear from Harding's telegrams that in all his talks with Makarios, the Archbishop was determined to be the sole arbiter of any ultimate settlement.

Nobody could feel very happy or sanguine about the situation as it then revealed itself. Yet neither Harding nor the Colonial Secretary, Alan Lennox-Boyd (now Lord Boyd), felt that we should abandon hope of an agreement. Not so Eden, who decided that the time had come for the British lion not only to roar at its adversary, but to gobble him up altogether. And on March 9, by order of the British Government, Archbishop Makarios was deported from Cyprus to the Seychelle Islands in the Pacific Ocean. Thus for the next year, until saner counsels prevailed and Makarios was released in March, 1957, the British Government deliberately removed from the scene the one and only man capable of negotiating an agreement on behalf of four-fifths of the Cypriot population. And it was not until February, 1959, after altogether more than three years of bloodshed amounting towards the end to virtual civil war between the Greek and Turkish communities, that Britain was able to extricate herself from an untenable situation, by granting independence to Cyprus which was to be guaranteed by both Greece and Turkey.

However, at the time these likely consequences of deporting Makarios were overlooked. Eden had made a stand in the name of British prestige and, although the Suez Group would have added the words 'at last', Conservative Members of Parliament were for the most part delighted by this demonstration that we were not going to be 'pushed around' any longer. Britain was acting like an imperial power again, they were able to tell their constituents. And as if to prove our status in the world, a few weeks later Marshal Bulganin and Mr. Khrushchev arrived in London for talks on the world situation in response to the invitation issued by Eden at the previous year's Summit Conference.

These talks produced no agreement on any of the topics discussed. But it was significant that Eden decided when they were over that the most important gain on our side lay in the discussions on the Middle East. Here he had told the Russian leaders bluntly and in words of one syllable that so vital to the British economy was the oil we obtained from the Middle East that 'we would fight for it' if the need arose. Eden had also raised the question of arms deliveries to the Arab states and had sought Russian acceptance of some limitation agreement. The Russians were not to be drawn on this, pointing out that the problem of regulating arms deliveries to the Middle East did not rest with Russia and Britain alone. But despite this evasive reply, Eden felt that progress had been made, in that both Governments understood that the Middle East was the area where Anglo-Russian differences were most likely to become acute. And he thought then—and has since confirmed in his book, *Full Circle*—that 'these discussions did something to put that danger at a further remove'. Yet within less than seven months he and members of his Government were to defend the Anglo-French invasion of Egypt in the Suez Crisis on the grounds that we had discovered a Russian plot to take over the Middle East and to eliminate all British influence from the area!

The next three months passed somewhat uneventfully and without offering any opportunity for Eden to translate his declaration of war on Nasser into action. Soon after Glubb's dismissal, Nasser announced that Egypt, Saudi Arabia and Syria were together prepared to replace any British assistance which might be withdrawn from Jordan with an annual subvention of £20 million. In the following month Egypt followed up this offer with the signature of a military pact with Saudi Arabia and Yemen. But King Hussein's immediate reaction to these Egyptian moves was to assure the British Ambassador that, now that Glubb had gone and with him the main focus of anti-British feeling in Jordan, he wanted to remain on the closest terms with Britain. He knew well enough that neither Egypt nor Syria could afford to take over the British subsidy and that the Saudis, as traditional enemies of the Hashemite dynasty, would be most unlikely to pay up. In fact, far from getting involved with Egypt at this point, Hussein promptly staged a meeting with his Hashemite cousin, King Feisal of Iraq, as a demonstration of solidarity between Iraq and Jordan.

Thus, with Jordan's King in a resistant mood and Iraq established as Britain's ally in the Baghdad Pact, there were for the time being no opportunities for Eden to rattle his sabre at his Egyptian enemy. And the most hostile gesture that he could make was to refuse to send a Minister to attend the celebrations in Cairo following the withdrawal of the last British forces from the Canal Zone on June 13. Aside from this, relations between Britain and Egypt continued on a normal footing. The flow, or perhaps I should say the trickle, of deliveries of obsolete and obsolescent British armaments to Egypt was maintained at an increased rate. Since the beginning of the year Egypt had been objecting to some of the terms of the Anglo-American loan for the Aswan Dam, which she claimed amounted to an attempt to control the Egyptian economy. (The ghosts of the Khedive Ismail and his European creditors seemed to be haunting the *coulisses* of the Egyptian Ministry of Finance!) But, all the same, discussions about the loan were continuing between Washington, London and Cairo.

Lloyd was also able to get Eden to agree to a more positive policy of help and support for Nuri in Iraq. Arguing that, as our ally in the Baghdad Pact, Nuri should receive special treatment, he persuaded them to step up the supply of arms to Iraq. Nuri was also encouraged to pursue his plans for a Fertile Crescent Union of Iraq, Syria and Jordan, a scheme for Arab unity which he had been nurturing for twenty years or more. Syria—as Nasser was to realise to his own horrified dismay eighteen months later—was being deeply penetrated by Communist influence and was undergoing a period of chronic instability, with *coups d'état* taking place every few months. And it seemed at the time that the Fertile Crescent project offered the best hope of stabilising her situation. However, as it turned out, Nuri's plans were frustrated, not by Russia, nor by Nasser, but rather by Saudi Arabia, who, fearing a powerful Hashemite-dominated combination on her borders, was prepared to pay more to keep Syria out of the Fertile Crescent than Nuri was willing to pay to bring her in.

This Saudi success in spiking Nuri's guns had inevitably unhappy repercussions on our relations with the successors of our former friend and ally, King Ibn Saud. We were currently involved in a bitter dipute with the Saudis over the Buraimi Oasis on the borders of Saudi Arabia and the British-protected Sultanate of Muscat and Oman on the Persian Gulf. Sniffing the possibility of a new oil strike in the area, the Saudis had seized Buraimi and proclaimed it to be part of their territory. They had soon been ejected by British troops and a long wrangle had followed in which the British Government had insisted that Buraimi was Omani territory and as such must be protected by Britain. The Americans, seeking to curry favour with the Saudis as landlords of their oil concessions at

Dahran, had tried hard to persuade us to compromise, but without success. Now, however, Azzam Pasha, the former Secretary-General of the Arab League and currently one of King Saud's advisers, had come to London to suggest to Selwyn Lloyd a possible settlement of the Buraimi dispute.

Azzam's suggestion was an arrangement whereby Saudi Arabia would be granted access to the eastern end of the Persian Gulf—which the existence of British-protected sheikhdoms all the way along the coast from Qatar to the Indian Ocean denied to her—and in return she would renounce her claims to Buraimi, which would remain part of Omani territory. Such an agreement, Azzam felt, would save King Saud's face while at the same time fulfilling our obligations to the Sultan of Muscat and Oman.

Selwyn Lloyd and I both warmly supported the project, which seemed to offer the prospect of removing a deep-seated irritant in our relations with the Saudis at a minimum cost to ourselves. We thought too that it would appeal to the Prime Minister as a means of drawing Saudi Arabia closer to us and hence away from Egypt. But how wrong we were. Eden turned Lloyd down flat. We had already surrendered too much in the Middle East, he claimed. Saudi Arabia was Nasser's ally and our enemy, not only on account of Buraimi, but also through her attempts to sabotage the Fertile Crescent. If we offered any concession for a Buraimi settlement, the Saudis would pocket it and then come back and ask for more. We must stand firm and insist on our rights—or, rather, those of the Sultan. The only thing that the Arabs understood was force, and until recently we had shown them too little of it.

In vain did Lloyd argue our need for friends in the Arab world. He was soundly defeated by Eden and the 'grape-shot' group among Ministers. The outcome could hardly have been more unhappy. The Buraimi dispute dragged on through the summer, a festering sore in Anglo-Saudi relations, until the British attack on Egypt in the autumn finally brought about the inevitable rupture.

However, depressing as this reaction to the Azzam plan undoubtedly was, at least we were able to get through the months of May and June without any further upheavals in Anglo-Egyptian relations which might have given Eden the opportunity to draw his sword. Nasser had given assurances to our Ambassador, Sir Humphrey Trevelyan, that radio attacks on Britain and her friends in the Arab world would be stopped, and for a while this was done. In June the last British troops left Egyptian soil, and with their departure a calm seemed to settle on the scene. But, as I knew all too well, it was a deceptive calm. Sooner or later an incident was bound to occur in that most explosive area which would give Eden the pretext that he sought to move in on Egypt and try to smash Nasser. As I packed my bags at the end of June to fly to a meeting of the Disarmament Commission in New York, I was filled with foreboding. And less than three weeks later Mr. John Foster Dulles, the American Secretary of State, was to set in motion a chain of events which provided the Prime Minister with his pretext, but which resulted in the destruction, not of Nasser, but of Eden himself.

4   Nationalisation of the Canal

My first inkling of these impending events came when I was dining privately one evening in my New York hotel with Cabot Lodge, the American Ambassador to the United Nations. Lodge then told me that he felt he should warn me that Dulles would in all probability shortly renege on the Aswan Dam loan. This was due largely to internal political problems. The Administration's foreign aid programme had recently run into serious trouble in Congress, where drastic cuts had been made. In this climate it would be courting a further rebuff to ask for an appropriation for the Aswan loan. Although the Government had tried hard to get back on terms with the Arab world after the damage done by President Truman's pro-Israeli policies, there were powerful anti-Arab, and more particularly anti-Egyptian, voices in Congress. Zionist influences were very strong and were continually at work belabouring the Government for letting Nasser get away with his blockade of the Suez Canal against Israeli shipping. And only a month before Egypt had upset the apple-cart still further by recognising Communist China. Now the Zionist lobby would be joined by the China lobby in opposing aid to Egypt, and with the presidential election coming along in less than four months, it just was not practical politics for the administration to go ahead and ask Congress to approve so large a loan to Egypt.

I duly reported this gloomy news to the Foreign Office, and a few days later, on July 19, Dulles sent for the Egyptian Ambassador to Washington and told him that the United States Government were backing out of the Aswan Dam loan. From London Eden promptly followed suit on behalf of the British Government. Nasser was at this point in Yugoslavia conferring with Marshal Tito and the Prime Minister of India, Pandit Nehru. And soon after his return to Egypt, in what seemed at the time to be a fit of pique over having been humiliated in front of the two leading figures in the neutralist world, he announced on July 26 the nationalisation of the Suez Canal Company, without so much as a word of prior consultation with the Arab League or with any of his Arab allies. (Nasser later told me that his decision was not dictated by anger so much as by a conviction that the cancellation of the Anglo-American loan for the Aswan Dam presaged a Western attempt to pressure him into making concessions to Israel over the Canal or possibly even a peace settlement on Israeli terms. The purpose of his dramatic reaction had therefore been to show that Egypt was not going to be pushed around by the West.)

By his action in nationalising the Anglo-French Company, Nasser anticipated by some twelve years the ending of the Suez Canal concession which had been granted by the Khedive Ismail in 1869 and was due to expire in 1968. Henceforth the management, maintenance and development of the Canal would be vested in the Egyptian Canal Authority; the former company and its stockholders would be fully compensated 'in accordance with the value of the shares shown on the Paris Stock Exchange on the day preceding the nationalisation decree'; and all officials and employees of the former company were to remain at their posts and carry on with their jobs under pain of imprisonment. (This last provision was not, in fact, enforced, and large numbers of Company pilots were allowed to walk out, no doubt to enable Egypt to show that Egyptian pilots could carry on every bit as efficiently as French.) In announcing this dramatic challenge, Nasser made great play with the sacrifices which Egypt had had to make for the Canal. He reminded his listeners of how Britain had forced the Khedive Ismail to hand over Egypt's 44 per cent. shareholding as part payment of his debts. He dwelt at length on the fact that, as a consequence of this usurious action, Egypt collected annually only £E1 million against the Anglo-French Company's total income of £E35 million. And he proclaimed that in future Egypt would collect all of those £E35 million and put the proceeds towards the cost of building the High Dam at Aswan which America and Britain had refused to help construct.

Today, ten years after the event, with record-breaking tonnages of shipping passing freely between Suez and Port Said under the direction and guidance of the Egyptian authority and Egyptian pilots, the reactions which greeted the nationalisation of the Canal throughout the Western world seem almost incredible. Yet at the time not only was there the wildest indignation on political grounds, but it was also seriously believed by intelligent men that under Egyptian management the whole system would grind to a halt in a year or so, the Canal would silt up and the greatest international waterway in the world, which carried twice as much tonnage as the Panama Canal, would become impassable to the world's shipping. Typical of this reaction was the comment of the London *Times* that, 'an international waterway of this kind cannot be worked by a nation of as low technical and managerial skills as the Egyptians'.

On legal grounds nationalisation was condemned—and with some justification—as a high-handed act of seizure against an international company, which would remove the international guarantee written into the Constantinople Convention of 1888, when the signatories recognised the Suez Canal Company as the effective operator and guarantor of free navigation in the Canal. Less than two years earlier the Egyptian representative at the U.N. had affirmed that the Company was an international enterprise and as such would continue to manage the Suez Canal. But now Nasser, pointing to the fact that under the terms of the Khedive's concessions the company was an Egyptian joint-stock company, contended that it could be nationalised without infringing international law. In fact, as frequently happens in international disputes, both arguments could be supported on legal grounds, which made it all the more necessary that the issue should be resolved by political and diplomatic negotiation and agreement.

But it was on the political aspects of the matter that the fiercest of reactions and the wildest of statements were forthcoming. Hugh Gaitskell, the leader of the Labour Opposition in the House of Commons, promptly denounced Nasser as another Hitler, and was warmly congratulated from the Government benches for his outspokenness. Herbert Morrison, who had been Labour Foreign Secretary at the time of the Persian oil crisis in 1951, followed suit with epithets about 'the pocket dictator in Cairo'. As for Eden himself, this was, of course, the challenge for which he had been waiting. Now at last he had found a pretext to launch an all-out campaign of political, economic and military pressures on Egypt and to destroy for ever Nasser's image as the leader of Arab nationalism.

It so happened that at the time of the Suez nationalisation King Feisal of Iraq was on a State visit to England, accompanied by his uncle, and former regent, Crown Prince Abdulillah, and by Nuri es-Said. In fact, all three of them were actually dining at No. 10 when the news arrived of Nasser's speech proclaiming the nationalisation of the Suez Canal Company. This was an unfortunate coincidence. For the Iraqis were, not surprisingly, nettled that Nasser should have failed to consult any fellow Arab state, even any of the oil-producing states, before embarking on a course of action that was bound to have serious political and economic repercussions on the whole Arab world. Inevitably, therefore, their reaction was more angry than cautious and Nuri, in particular, expressed the hope that Britain would respond resolutely to Nasser's act of defiance.

In the light of subsequent events, it is only fair to Nuri's

memory to say that he later told me that he had also warned
Eden to resist any temptation to ally himself with Israel, or with
France, in order to bring Nasser to heel, since any such alliance
would have dire results for Anglo-Arab relations. But, not
knowing this at the time, whenever I came to counsel caution,
Eden was able to retort that he had the backing of Iraq, and
no doubt other Arab states as well, for his pressure tactics
against Egypt.

Thus fortified by Nuri's advice, the Prime Minister issued
his orders for the campaign of economic and military pressures
against Egypt to be started. Two days after the nationalisation
of the Canal, the Treasury ordered that all Egypt's sterling
balances and assets should be frozen. France followed suit on
July 29 and the United States did likewise two days later. On
July 30 Eden ordered a ban on the export of all further war
material to Egypt; four days later some 20,000 British Army
reservists were called up, and naval, military and air reinforcements were despatched to the eastern Mediterranean. Eden
telegraphed to President Eisenhower to say that economic pressures alone were 'unlikely to attain our objectives' and that he
and his colleagues were 'convinced that we must be ready, in
the last resort, to use force to bring Nasser to his senses'. The
Chiefs of Staff, Eden added, had been instructed 'to prepare a
military plan accordingly'. With these ominous words the
American President was invited to exchange views with
the British and French governments on the best means of un-
doing Nasser's action and placing the management of the Canal
once more in international custody. Two days later Eden went
a stage further and, as Eisenhower has revealed in his book
Waging Peace, sent the President a very secret message saying that he had decided that the only way to break Nasser would
be to resort to force without delay and without attempting to
negotiate. To this Eisenhower responded by sending Dulles
to London with instructions to promote the earliest practicable
meeting of the maritime powers with a view to bringing Nasser
to negotiate a reasonable settlement. At the same time, he tele-

graphed to Eden his grave misgivings about the decision to use force straight away, which would 'outrage' American as well as world opinion.

Meanwhile, the French Government was denouncing Nasser's action as comparable to Hitler's reoccupation of the Rhineland in the thirties. And as the wires began to hum between London and Paris about the seizure of the Anglo-French company, Eden began to ally himself more and more closely with his French counterpart, Guy Mollet. In the days following the end of World War II, when France looked to Britain to hold her hand against a reviving Germany as a pre-condition of French acceptance of German rearmament, whether in the abortive project for a European Army or as a member of N.A.T.O., Eden had had little use for this former schoolmaster who had become the leader of the French Socialist Party. Mollet was always moaning, he then said, about Britain's lack of sympathy for France. But now Eden recognised that a strong bond of common interest united him with Mollet, who believed that with Nasser out of the way the insurrection of the Algerian nationalists, which had been going on for two years, would die a natural death and Algeria would then peaceably accept the blessings of French colonial rule.

There was, of course, one grave danger in this growing Anglo-French partnership—the existence of a close alliance of France and Israel. But when I pointed this out to Eden, he brushed me aside, saying that I was a prisoner of the anti-Israel prejudice in the Foreign Office. He refused to listen to my warnings that the French might involve us with the Israelis, whose obvious interests lay in control of the Canal and of the terminal ports of Suez and Port Said being taken out of Nasser's hands. Eden now took the line that France had a justifiable grievance against Nasser over Algeria, as had Israel over the Suez Canal and the Arab blockade. Forgetting the view he had expressed to me in Berlin two years before that Egypt had a case under the Constantinople Convention for refusing passage through the Canal to ships of a nation with whom she was in a state of war, he now contended that Israeli shipping had been unjustly barred from using an international waterway and that Britain and France must help to restore to Israel her rights of passage. Nasser was the sworn enemy of Israel, and of France and Britain too, and if he were allowed to keep sole control of the Canal he would be stimulated to step up his pressure against Israel and to interfere with British or French shipping in the Canal.

I pointed out that he could do all this before he nationalised the Canal Company, since the terminal ports were Egyptian territory and under Egyptian control. Besides, why would he stop British or French shipping now that he stood to collect all the dues from ships transitting the Canal? Eden merely replied that I should know that the capacity of the Arabs to cut off their nose to spite their face was infinite. But it was as clear as daylight that behind his answer lay the hope that Nasser would now overstep the mark and prevent the passage of a British ship. And it was with this hope in mind that he and Mollet decided that henceforth all British and French shipping companies should pay their Canal dues to the former Company's account in London or Paris and should refuse to pay anything to the new Egyptian Canal Authority.

Unfortunately for Eden and his French partner, the effect of these measures was not what they hoped. Nasser was not to be led into their carefully baited trap, and throughout the next three months, until the Canal was blocked following the Israeli invasion of Sinai, British, French and other shipping continued to pass without let or hindrance between Port Said and Suez. Still more aggravating for those who wanted to settle with Nasser by the use of force rather than by negotiation, these economic sanctions, combined with growing political pressures from Egypt's Arab League associates, succeeded three months later in inducing Nasser to concede terms which Selwyn Lloyd was to describe as offering an acceptable compromise. But because neither Eden nor Mollet then wanted any compromise and because they insisted on using force, these terms were to become a dead letter. And when the use of force failed to achieve their objective, all hope of restoring some element of international control over the Suez Canal had to be abandoned.

Western Reactions

On August 1 Mr. Dulles arrived in London to take part in the talks between Britain, France and the United States which had begun a couple of days earlier. He lost no time in saying that he was in full agreement with Eden's statement in the House of Commons that no arrangements for the Suez Canal's future would be acceptable 'which would leave it in the unfettered control of a single power which could . . . exploit it purely for purposes of national policy'. And to Eden's delight, he spoke of finding a way 'to make Nasser disgorge'. He even admitted the possibility of using force, although only in the very last resort and after all other methods had failed.

Although the immediate result was to persuade Eden at least to go through the motions of attempting to mobilise world opinion in favour of an international sanction before resorting to more forceful measures, there is no doubt that Dulles' words were unfortunately chosen. For they undoubtedly encouraged Eden to believe that, notwithstanding Eisenhower's cautionary cable, the United States were a lot more solidly behind Britain and France than was the case, or could possibly be the case, with a presidential election looming in three months' time. And for Dulles to mislead his two allies at this stage was as unwise and dangerous as were his later attempts to restrain Britain and France from forcing the issue. Dulles and Eden had never liked or trusted each other. This was due partly to a mutual jealousy between two acknowledged experts in international affairs and partly to the fact that Dulles had not been altogether straightforward in his dealings with Britain's Labour Government over the Japanese Peace Treaty when he was serving as an adviser on the American delegation. This had led Eden to tell Eisenhower, before he became President, that he hoped that Dulles would not become Eisenhower's Secretary of State, as he felt that he could not work with him. And throughout the four years that Dulles and Eden were to play opposite one another on the international stage, they seldom showed any real confidence in each other's statements or actions, even on issues where there was total agreement both on principle and on method between America and Britain. Thus when it came to the crunch over Suez, where Dulles wished to play the honest broker, while Eden wanted to play the bold warrior, the two men were to end up as the bitterest of enemies, each blaming the other for the failure of his chosen role.

At the outset of the Suez affair, however, appearances suggested more or less complete unity of purpose between America, Britain and France. And in this spirit of seeming harmony the three governments agreed to call a conference of the original signatories of the Constantinople Convention, together with the other principal maritime nations and users of the Canal. But Eden's idea of the purpose of such a conference was fundamentally different from that of Dulles. And it is no exaggeration to say that whereas Dulles hoped for at least a basis for negotiations, in his heart Eden hoped that the conference would produce a solution unacceptable to Nasser, which tragic truth dawned upon the Americans too late for them to prevent the inevitable disaster.

From the beginning events played into Eden's hands. Egypt refused to attend the conference on the grounds that its object was to put the clock back and to reinstate the former Canal Company or its replica. Nasser also declined to negotiate any settlement under the threat of the Anglo-French troop concentrations that were then taking place in the Eastern Mediterranean. Thus the conference, when it met on August 16, did so without the participation of the only defendant in the dispute and with a built-in majority of the Western Powers and their friends and allies. Such a gathering, meeting in such circumstances, was hardly likely to produce a solution acceptable to Nasser even as a basis for negotiation, at any rate until the denial of Canal dues to Egypt and the pressures of the Arab League had had time to take effect.

In the event, eighteen of the twenty-two nations attending the conference brushed aside the efforts of the Indian delegation to suggest a compromise and agreed, against the opposition of Russia, Indonesia, India and Ceylon, to propose that the operation of the Canal should be entrusted to an international board. This body was to include the Egyptians and the principal users of the Canal. In other words, the management was to be handed over to an agency largely dominated by the Western Powers, with Egypt in a permanent minority position. And to make the whole idea still more unpalatable to Nasser, in an obvious allusion to the question of Israeli shipping, the Eighteen-Power proposals insisted that the board should ensure that the Canal was operated 'without political motivation in favour of, or in prejudice against, any user'. Mr. (now Sir) Robert Menzies, the Prime Minister of Australia, was appointed by the eighteen nations to head a delegation to Cairo to convey these propositions to the Egyptian Government.

Menzies arrived in Cairo on September 3 and for the next six days tried every argument to persuade Nasser to accept the idea of an international board. But to no avail. To his contention that a grave international situation had been created by the nationalisation of the Canal, Nasser retorted that he was not responsible. He had a perfect legal right, he claimed, to nationalise the Suez Canal Company, and it was the 'threats' of Britain and France which had created the grave situation. Nothing would induce him to consider any solution which derogated from Egypt's absolute right to run the Canal as an

Egyptian national undertaking. The Eighteen-Power proposal challenged that right and sought to reimpose foreign domination over Egypt, and he would have none of it. As for insulating the Canal from politics, the idea was quite unreal. For, with the terminal ports under Egyptian control, Egypt had always had, and must always have, the right to protect her own security. (Nasser could have added that, when towards the end of the nineteenth century the European Powers proposed that the Canal be subject to international control, it was Britain who insisted that nothing should be done to limit her freedom of action in Egypt.) Menzies tried hard to persuade Nasser that he was in essence being asked to accept the position of a landlord, with an international tenant, or tenants, holding a lease, which in no way derogated from his right of ownership. But it was no use; Nasser remained adamant. And on September 9 the Australian Prime Minister was forced to admit complete failure.

Nasser had done what Eden expected of him and the stage appeared to be set for Britain and France to force his hand by the use of military sanctions. But Eden and Mollet now found themselves confronted by two seemingly insuperable difficulties. In the first place, Nasser had offered no real provocation that would justify the use of force. He had seized an Anglo-French Company, but he had not done any injury to British or French lives, nor had he stopped a British or French ship passing through the Canal, despite the refusal of the owners to pay dues to the Egyptian Canal Authority. The second problem confronting the British and French Governments lay in the discovery that 'Operation Musketeer', as the plan of the Chiefs of Staff for military action against Egypt was called, could not be carried out at short notice. The absence of a deep-water port in Cyprus meant that the bulk of any invasion force had to come from Malta, 1,000 miles from Egypt. Apart from bombing operations, Cyprus could be used only for the despatch of paratroops; and even with the addition of the sizeable airborne forces possessed by the French, it was impossible to muster more than one paratroop division. Such a force could not be asked to seize and hold the Canal from Port Said to Suez without strong sea-borne reinforcements.

Thus even if Nasser could be goaded into an act of provocation, there could be no question of Britain and France smashing him with a swift and sudden blow. Yet Eden's craving for some quick success that would raise Britain's prestige had to be satisfied somehow. And, finding himself thus frustrated over Egypt, he now turned on the E.O.K.A. resistance movement in Cyprus. About this time the E.O.K.A. leader, Grivas, had offered publicly to stop all terrorist activities and to permit a ceasefire to allow an opportunity for progress to be made with the constitutional advance offered by the British Government earlier in the year. Instead of seizing on this opportunity to bring Makarios back to Cyprus and to pin him down to further talks about a settlement in an atmosphere no longer permeated with terrorism, Eden hailed the Grivas offer as an indication that E.O.K.A. were cracking under the strain imposed by British security measures and responded accordingly. E.O.K.A. was offered the alternative of laying down their arms and being deported or facing extermination at the hands of the British forces in Cyprus. This offer was, of course, rejected and in the next few months E.O.K.A. was to show that, far from being on the run, it could excel in violence anything that had been done since the rebellion started.

Meanwhile, the French Government, having no E.O.K.A. against which they could vent their wrath, kept on pegging away with their efforts to topple Nasser. There was nothing that they could do to remove the logistic obstacles to a quick military operation. But if the British were squeamish about attacking Nasser without provocation, there were ways of manufacturing the necessary pretext. Without saying a word at this point to Eden, or to any British Minister, the French had turned to the Israelis for help in this direction. Israel had recently been complaining bitterly about raids across her borders conducted by Egyptian-sponsored terrorists, the so-called *feda-*

yeen; and Mollet and his Ministers realised instinctively that with a little encouragement it should be possible to turn the current Israeli temper to French advantage.

France had been in the closest contact with Israel ever since the 1954 agreement between Britain and Egypt had heralded the early withdrawal of British forces from the Suez Canal Zone. Israel, claiming that this withdrawal left her more than ever exposed to Egypt's threats, had then sought aid and comfort from the French, who, having lost out to Arab nationalism in Lebanon and Syria, and being threatened with a similar fate in North Africa, were bitterly anti-Arab, and especially anti-Egyptian. The French had responded both with sympathy and, in a more practical sense, with arms. Little did they care if they flouted the balance-of-arms policy of the signatories of the Tripartite Declaration. And, in their cynical way, they did not even care that the large quantities of French arms sold to Israel should have precipitated the arms deal between Egypt and the Soviet bloc. This, they reasoned, would only encourage Nasser to overstep the mark and so bring about his own destruction. Thus as I was later to discover, it happened that, when Nasser nationalised the Canal Company, the Director-General of the Israeli Ministry of Defence, Mr. Shimon Peres, was engaged in discussing arms deliveries with the French Government. And even while Menzies was still in Cairo trying to persuade Nasser to negotiate on the Eighteen-Power proposals, the French were hard at work with Peres and Israeli staff officers planning a method of recapturing the Canal with Israeli assistance.

I was away on sick-leave during the early part of August, and only returned when the London Conference had ended and Menzies was about to take off for Cairo. At the first opportunity I confessed my anxieties both to Eden and to Lloyd about the course on which we were embarked. I pointed out all the obvious dangers of allying ourselves too closely with France, and therefore with Israel, the two nations most hated and suspected by the Arabs. I urged that we should keep in the closest touch with the Americans and I suggested that, unless by some miracle Menzies managed to persuade Nasser to negotiate on the Eighteen-Power proposal, our next step should be to go to the U.N. The spontaneous reaction of anger on the part of the British public, which followed the nationalisation of the Canal, was now subsiding. Gaitskell seemed to be weakening in his support of the 'tough' line and, if only to hold him to a bi-partisan approach, it was essential that we refer the question to the Security Council and, if that resulted in a Russian veto, ask for a special meeting of the General Assembly to pronounce in our favour.

Eden's reply to all this was blunt. If we did not show strength now, we should eventually lose all our oil to Nasser. The Americans did not really care about the Suez Canal, but the French did, and so did the Israelis, who deserved to be allowed to use it. He did not care whether Gaitskell supported or opposed him. As for the U.N., they had proved to be a dead loss; neither the Security Council nor the General Assembly could give us what we wanted. And when I retorted that, while the U.N. would obviously not give us Nasser's head on a charger, they could give massive support to a compromise settlement, Eden reverted to his theme that compromise with Nasser would only serve to whet his appetite and that I must get it into my head that this man must be destroyed before he destroyed all of us.

Lloyd took a rather different line. While agreeing with Eden that Nasser posed a grave threat to British interests in the Middle East, he told me that he was arguing strongly that, when the Menzies mission had failed to get a settlement by direct negotiation, we should go straight to the U.N. Whatever we decided to do in the end, he said, whether we continued to negotiate or moved in to settle the issue by force of arms, we must first go through the U.N. hoop. 'We must set the stage,' he concluded. And when I asked if his stage-setting would be for war, he replied, 'For war or for negotiation.' I pressed him to say which course he favoured. But he avoided a direct answer, merely saying that he felt sure that Nasser would in due time commit some act of provocation. With the French and ourselves and most of the other principal Canal users, except the Americans, paying our dues to the former Company's account in London and Paris, Nasser was being denied some 65 per cent. of the income which he had hoped to gain by nationalisation. He could not tolerate this indefinitely, and sooner or later he would decide to stop a British or French ship and seize it for non-payment of dues to Egypt. That would give us a *casus belli*.

A few days after these gloomy conversations my hopes rose when Lloyd told me that he had persuaded his colleagues to refer the issue to the U.N., provided the French agreed. But my hopes were soon to be dashed to the ground. For when the French were approached, they accepted only on condition that the United States and a majority of the Security Council should undertake in advance of the debate to defeat any attempt to bind them and us not to resort to force if we failed to get satisfaction from the U.N. Inevitably the United States Government refused to give any such guarantee. And Dulles, contending that there was not sufficient unity of approach between the French, the Americans and ourselves to risk exposure to the divisive tactics of the Russians in the Security Council, decided that this was not the time to take the issue to the U.N.

The Americans had been put on notice that Britain and France wanted to settle the issue by force, and not just as a last resort, and they were not going to be parties to such a course of action. From now on, therefore, our paths were to drift apart until final breaking-point was reached some eight weeks later.

6   Dulles *v*. Eden

With the parting of the ways between Britain and the United States, Dulles embarked on a course of action which was doomed to become self-defeating. Although possessing a brilliant brain as well as a remarkable grasp of international affairs, Dulles was much too inflexible to be able to deal with Eden at this crucial juncture. Had he been less unbending, he would have seen that his best hope of preventing Eden from going to war was to do what Eden himself had done at the Geneva Conference on Indo-China in 1954. There the roles had been reversed and it was the Americans who wanted to settle the issue with the North Vietnamese Communists and their Chinese allies by force of arms, while Eden saw that the only answer was to negotiate. Eden had accordingly taken the initiative in forming a diplomatic pressure group sufficiently powerful and influential to force the Communists to accept a compromise. He had even won for his efforts the support of the Russians, then far more closely allied to Communist China than they are today. And at the end of the day he had brought about a settlement which the Americans were compelled to acknowledge.

But instead of copying Eden's tactics over Indo-China, Dulles from now on seemed to be desperately trying to hold on to Eden's coat-tails. And every move that he made and every suggestion that he offered seemed to Eden to be designed to compel him to abandon the use of force, rather than to bring Nasser to negotiate a settlement. Such tactics inevitably had the opposite effect to what he intended. Never having trusted Dulles, Eden decided that he was more on Egypt's side than on Britain's. And so he concluded that Britain, together with France, would have to go it alone.

Having turned down the suggestion of a reference to the U.N., Dulles felt obliged to come up with an alternative proposal. He now suggested that a Suez Canal Users' Association should be formed. The precise purpose of this body was not explained at the time, although Dulles rather vaguely indicated that it should stand ready to organise navigation, hire pilots and generally supervise the management of the Canal. But since such an arrangement would have been even more disagreeable to Egypt than the Eighteen-Power proposal which Menzies had failed to get Nasser to accept, no really precise definition of the purposes of the S.C.U.A. was agreed. This was to cause much subsequent misunderstanding and confusion, the more so since Dulles, when presenting his suggestion to Lloyd, argued that it was deliberately designed to show Nasser that, if he rejected the Eighteen-Power proposal, he could not expect terms as good in the future.

On this assurance, Eden accepted the S.C.U.A. project. At least a Users' Club, he told himself, could do no harm. And it could be a means of keeping together the eighteen Powers who wanted to make Nasser 'disgorge', and of establishing a holding agency, into whose coffers its members should pay their Canal dues. The Americans, despite the strongest pressures from Britain and France, had still not come into line over the denial of dues to Egypt, on the grounds that they could not dictate to their shipowners, still less to the large number of American ships flying the Liberian or Panamanian flag. And it seemed at the time that the formation of such a body might provide that extra bit of pressure required to bring the Americans into line with the majority of the maritime Powers who were paying their dues in London or Paris.

However, no sooner had the S.C.U.A. project been accepted in London and put to the other members of the Eighteen-Power group, than a couple of statements emanating from across the Atlantic revealed a wide gulf between the American and British attitudes. Eisenhower was asked, at a Press conference on September 11, whether America would back Britain and France if they resorted to force against Egypt. Obviously taken aback by this blunt enquiry, he replied that 'this country will not go to war ever while I am occupying my present post unless the Congress ... declares such a war'. And, following this up, Dulles stated two days later that even if Egypt used force over the Canal, 'we do not intend to shoot our way through'. And he went on to say that, so far as he understood Eden's position, 'I did not get the impression that there was any undertaking or pledge given by him to shoot their way through the Canal'.

It would be impossible to imagine a statement more likely to exasperate Eden. To his way of thinking, Eisenhower's answer had been 'weak' enough, although it had the justification that it reflected the constitutional position of the U.S. President. But Dulles had gone much further. He had not only said that America would turn the other cheek to Nasser, but also suggested that Britain might do likewise. To make matters worse, he had said all this in the middle of a difficult two-day emergency debate in the House of Commons. Eden was in an extremely awkward position. On the one hand, the Suez Group of Conservative M.P.s were vociferously urging that strong-arm methods be employed to deal with the 'dictator Nasser'. On the other, Gaitskell and the Labour Opposition, having greatly changed their tune since the debates following the nationalisation of the Canal, were now pressing the Government to submit the issue to the U.N. and to give an undertaking that they would not use force, except with U.N. authority, or at least until the Security Council had failed to provide satisfaction. Gaitskell and his colleagues suggested that the Government's reluctance to refer the issue to the U.N. was due to their fear of being asked, as part of their contribution to a settlement, to call off the military movements with which they and the French were currently threatening Egypt.

Not being aware of the contacts and conspiracies that were being pursued between representatives of the French and Israeli General Staffs, Eden could not at this juncture see how it would be possible to use force, unless Nasser struck the first blow. And Nasser was showing no sign of obliging him on this score. Yet he rebelled at the idea of giving any pledge not to use force pending discussion in the Security Council. The Russians would in all probability help him by vetoing any resolution which rehearsed the Eighteen-Power proposals. But there was no guarantee that some nation—very possibly the United States—would not seek to entangle Britain and France in a compromise motion which would make it difficult or even impossible to use force, should a pretext arise at a later stage. Dulles' earlier refusal to meet the French request on this point signalled a real danger that he might attempt such a blocking manœuvre. Thus Eden rejected the Opposition's demands, ignoring Gaitskell's offer not to divide the House if the Government would agree to refer the issue unconditionally to the U.N. And with the ensuing division, the last hope of maintaining a bi-partisan approach to the Suez dispute went out of the window.

Six days later, on September 19, a second conference of maritime nations met in London to consider the American plan for a Users' Club. From the outset a wide difference of purpose was evident between the American and British approaches. On Eden's instructions, Lloyd made it clear that Britain looked to the S.C.U.A. as a means of denying Canal dues to Egypt and, to this end, he tried hard to get words written into the Association's terms of reference which would bind all members to pay their dues to its account, and not to the Egyptian Canal Authority. But Dulles, fearing that this might stimulate Nasser to an act of provocation, insisted that membership of S.C.U.A. 'would not involve the assumption by any member of any obligation'. He preferred a form of words which would only require members 'voluntarily to take such action with respect to their ships and payment of Canal dues as would facilitate the work of the Association'.

Far from making things tougher for Nasser, as Dulles had contended was his purpose, this new American approach suggested that the Users' Club would do no more than crystallise the *status quo* and would not be empowered to bring any further pressure on Egypt. And all Dulles' earlier fine phrases about creating an association to 'promote safe, orderly, efficient and economical transit of member-controlled vessels' through the Canal now seemed to have been forgotten. The best that Lloyd could get on the crucial issue of dues was a purely permissive clause in the Association's constitution which invited it 'to receive, hold and disburse the revenues accruing from dues and other sums which any user of the Canal may pay to the Association . . . pending a final settlement'. And those shipowners who were still paying dues to Egypt were to be asked voluntarily to consent to paying them to S.C.U.A.

In this somewhat emasculated form, agreement was reached among the eighteen Powers to set up the Suez Canal Users' Association and to hold its inaugural meeting in London on October 1. Although Nasser denounced this development as an 'association for waging war' and an unjustifiable attempt to infringe Egypt's sovereign rights, it was inevitably, and from the outset, a feeble project. Looking back on these events, one is drawn irresistibly to the conclusion that, by his negative attitude at the Second London Conference, Dulles threw away the best opportunity he ever had of getting out in front of Eden and placing himself at the head of a real pressure group designed to bring Britain, France and Egypt to negotiate a settlement. Whether he intended it as such or not, his idea of a Users' Club contained the essence of such a grouping, provided that its members all bound themselves to pay their dues to the Club's account. But because he allowed fear to be his counsellor—fear of provoking Nasser to provoke Eden and the French—Dulles destroyed his own initiative and with it his power to influence events or prevent the tragedy which followed.

7

Breach with America

When it became clear that the S.C.U.A. project was not going to turn out as Eden had hoped, Lloyd once again got to work on his colleagues with his theme of 'setting the stage' by a reference to the United Nations. Dulles was still unenthusiastic about going to the Security Council in a state of evident disarray among the Western Powers. But several of the representatives of the eighteen Powers had stressed during the Second London Conference that it would greatly help them to persuade public opinion at home that they were right in supporting Britain and France, if we were now to take the issue to the U.N. Besides, there was the ever-present danger that the Russians might forestall us in the Security Council and, by raising the Suez dispute themselves, get a resolution passed which called on Britain and France to stop threatening Egypt. And finally there was, as Lloyd saw it, the constant nagging of the Labour Party on this aspect, which could not be altogether ignored.

So distraught was Eden at the turn which events had taken that, although he had no love and still less respect for the U.N. as a court of justice, he was persuaded by Lloyd's arguments and agreed to ask for a meeting of the Security Council early in October. Anything, he felt, was better than merely sitting back and waiting while our case went by default and Nasser 'consolidated his prize'. British public opinion was becoming apathetic, the reservists were getting restive and there was no sign as yet that our economic pressures on Egypt were giving Nasser pause. Accordingly, the French Government was asked to join with us in requesting a Security Council debate for October 3, two days after the proposed inauguration of S.C.U.A. This time Mollet agreed without conditions, and on September 23 an Anglo-French note was sent to the President of the Security Council asking that the Suez dispute be placed on the Council's agenda. The Americans were invited to join in this initiative, but Dulles, now thoroughly suspicious of our motives, declined.

Three days later, on September 26, Eden and Lloyd flew to Paris for talks with Mollet and Pineau. Before they left, Eden sent for me and told me to explore with the European experts at the Foreign Office whether there was any 'present' that he might take with him which would demonstrate our desire for Anglo-French solidarity. Mollet had had an extraordinary success for a post-war Prime Minister of France and had already lasted longer than any of his recent predecessors. And Eden wanted to help him to stay in office. To my astonishment, he suggested that the Foreign Office should have another look at Churchill's offer of common citizenship for all British and French nationals, which was made in 1940 in a desperate effort to keep France in the fight against Hitler. I replied that it seemed hardly appropriate to revive such an offer at this stage, and that the best gesture we could make would be to join in the negotiations for a European Common Market which had started at Messina fifteen months before and from which we had deliberately absented ourselves. Mollet had wanted us to join in the European Coal and Steel Community and in the abortive project for a European Army, and the best 'present' we could offer him was to declare ourselves ready to enter the incipient Common Market.

But Eden, who disliked the idea of getting entangled with any European movement which smacked of federation, would have none of this. He wanted to offer the French something special, some gesture of particular significance to the Anglo-French alliance, and not something which France would have to share with five other European countries. Would I therefore please do as I was bid and look at the possibilities of reviving the Churchill offer?

In the event, nothing came of this strange notion and Eden left for Paris with no 'present' for Mollet. But as things turned out, he need not have worried his head about bolstering up the French Prime Minister, who at this moment was not only firmly established in office, but also highly delighted with the course of the Franco-Israeli staff talks. And when Eden and Lloyd reached Paris, they found Mollet and Pineau in great spirits and in a very belligerent mood. So certain were they that the Israelis would shortly provide the pretext for settling the Canal issue by force that they no longer showed any qualms about going to the U.N. or establishing the Users' Club, both of which they regarded as necessary preliminaries for the forth-coming military operations. But they did not at this stage reveal to Eden or Lloyd the plans which they were concocting with the Israelis. And for the moment they contented themselves with whole-heartedly endorsing Eden's contention that, if the Security Council failed to agree upon a just solution, Britain and France should be ready to use whatever measures, including force, might be needed to resolve the dispute.

Still knowing nothing of the 'ace' which Mollet had up his sleeve, Eden returned to London only a very little less depressed than when he left. Of one thing he felt certain: that if S.C.U.A. was to be anything more than window-dressing, the Americans must be persuaded to fall into line on the payment of Canal dues. The more difficult the prospect of staging 'Operation Musketeer' became, the more imperative it was to bring maximum economic pressure to bear on Nasser. The United States Government had finally agreed to ask the owners of ships flying the American flag to pay their dues to the S.C.U.A. account, but the large fleets sailing under Panamanian and Liberian register were not included. Accordingly, soon after his return from Paris, Eden cabled to Eisenhower on October 1 yet another appeal to be firm with Nasser and to find a way for all American ships, irrespective of flag, to withhold payment of dues from Egypt. Nasser, he contended, was to Russia what Mussolini had been to Hitler, and Russia was the real danger in the Middle East. The Soviet Government had been loud in their support of Nasser's act of piracy and, both in public and in diplomatic notes, they had denounced every action taken by Britain and France since nationalisation as provocative and threatening towards Egypt and as likely to endanger peace.

But Eden's efforts to bring the Americans into line by parading the Communist bogy were to no avail. Dulles was now convinced that Britain and France wanted war with Egypt. Rumours had begun to reach the Central Intelligence Agency that France and Israel were in cahoots and that large quantities of French military equipment had been promised to the Israelis. And Dulles was thoroughly frightened by these rumours. Accordingly, on the very day after Eden had sent his appeal to Eisenhower, the Secretary of State held a Press conference at which he went out of his way to dissociate the Government of the United States from Britain and France. There were differences, he said, between the three governments arising 'from fundamental concepts'. In the N.A.T.O. area they were at one, but in areas outside, 'encroaching in some form of manner on the problem of so-called colonialism', the United States was to be found 'playing a somewhat independent role'. Then, going on to speak more specifically of the Suez Canal Users' Association, he said in reply to a question: 'There is talk about teeth being pulled out of the plan, but I know of no teeth. There were no teeth in it, so far as I am aware.'

I was at No. 10 Downing Street when the news-flash of Dulles' Press conference came across the tapes. Eden's private secretary brought it in at the very moment when I was pleading

with the Prime Minister not to get too far out of step with the
United States and not to despair of carrying them with us both
in the Security Council and subsequently. Eden read the Dulles
statement quickly and then, with a contemptuous gesture, he
flung the piece of paper at me across the table, hissing as he
did so, 'And now what have you to say for your American
friends?'

I had no answer. For I knew instinctively that this was for
Eden the final let-down. We had reached breaking-point. Up
to now several Ministers had been clearly concerned about
the Prime Minister's 'go-it-alone' policy, so long as there was
the slightest hope of getting the Americans to form a firm front
with us. But now, I could see that the last chance of retrieving
an Anglo-American understanding had been lost. I knew that
henceforth Eden would be able to count on the overwhelming
majority of his Government for settling the issue by force,
irrespective of what the Americans might say. Dulles had provided him with an alibi which none of his colleagues would
feel able to challenge.

The loud cries of British protest which poured into the State
Department following Dulles' statement were not, however,
without effect on the American Secretary of State. And when
Lloyd and he met in New York for the Security Council session, Dulles hastened to deny that he was at cross-purposes
with Britain and France in anything save the use of force. The
current rumours that he favoured an Indian proposal for a revision of the Constantinople Convention, which would recognise Egypt's rights to own and operate the Canal, were not true,
he claimed. He still stood firmly by the principle of international
control and he felt certain that this would in the end be accepted by Nasser. Egypt's position was deteriorating; Nasser
would not be able to hold out indefinitely; and if we could be
patient for a little while longer, Egypt would be forced in the

end to accept the principle of international supervision of the Canal.

Eden pooh-poohed all this as just another delaying device invented by America to sabotage his efforts to win a just settlement. When I suggested that Dulles could be right and that perhaps the pressures on Egypt were having more effect than our information had led us to think, he retorted that it was clear as daylight that Nasser was consolidating his position, and that the longer we delayed getting to grips with him, the stronger and more arrogant he would become. Dulles believed that he could negotiate with Nasser on a basis of sweet reasonableness; but all our experience had proved the contrary. If Menzies had failed, Dulles could not succeed, except by surrendering every point of principle. Nasser was unnegotiable, as I would shortly see from the Egyptian reaction to the resolution calling for a just and peaceful settlement which we and the French were going to table in the Security Council.

In fact, what emerged from the proceedings of the Security Council and still more from the talks which were to be held behind the scenes between Lloyd, Pineau, Fawzi, the Egyptian Foreign Minister, and Dag Hammarskjöld revealed a very different state of affairs to that forecast by Eden. As Dulles had suggested, Egypt's position was being seriously weakened by the combination of pressures which Nasser's precipitate action had brought upon him. And, to say the very least, the discussions in New York produced the makings of an agreement on the future of the Suez Canal which Lloyd felt at the time, and later publicly admitted, gave us substantially what we required in the way of guarantees that the Canal would be operated in the interests of all who used it.

8

Egyptian Concessions

The Security Council met on October 5. A procedural wrangle promptly ensued as to whether an Egyptian complaint about British and French troop movements should take precedence over the Anglo-French submission. After a brief discussion, this was resolved in favour of Britain and France. Selwyn Lloyd then led off the main debate with a demand for a general endorsement of the S.C.U.A. plan, and of the Eighteen-Power proposals. 'The whole future of the rule of law and respect for international obligations is in jeopardy', he stated. 'That strikes at the foundation of the new system of international society that we are seeking so painstakingly to construct.' And after rehearsing our requirements for international control over the Canal, he went on to bid for U.N. support by stressing that he set great store by the part which the United Nations would play in the new Canal régime.

The requirements stated by Lloyd, later to be known as the Six Principles and to be incorporated in the Anglo-French resolution of October 13, were the following:

1. There should be free and open transmit through the Canal without discrimination, overt or covert.

2. The sovereignty of Egypt should be respected.

3. The operation of the Canal should be insulated from the politics of any country.

4. The manner of fixing tolls and charges should be decided by agreement between Egypt and the users.

5. A fair proportion of the dues should be allotted to development.

6. In case of disputes, unresolved affairs between the Suez Canal Company and the Egyptian Government should be settled by arbitration.

As the Egyptian reaction was shortly to show, this much was perfectly acceptable. But when it came to deciding by what method the Six Principles were to be translated into practice, Lloyd sought to insist on the establishment of the International Board which had formed the basis of the Eighteen-Power proposals. As the Americans pointed out behind the scenes, this reversion to what Nasser had already rejected out of hand was courting an Egyptian rebuff and a Russian veto. Moreover, to Dulles' way of thinking, the idea seemed to have been largely superseded by the newer concept of a Users' Club. Nevertheless, in an effort to repair some of the damage done to Anglo-American relations by his public utterances, Dulles gave Lloyd his full backing in the debate. But the Russian Foreign Minister, Mr. Shepilov, opposed the British suggestion and insisted that a six-power commission be established to negotiate a revised Suez Canal Convention. Once again it seemed the Security Council would be deadlocked.

However, at this point the Egyptians, instead of following Russia's negative suit, showed a surprising desire for a compromise. Fawzi announced that in the view of his Government the basis of any negotiations should rest on three principles. These were, first, the establishment of a system of co-operation between Egypt and the users of the Canal which would take account both of Egypt's sovereign rights and of the users' interests; second, a system of tolls and charges which guaranteed fair treatment and no exploitation; and, third, the earmarking of a reasonable portion of the Canal revenues for development and improvement.

This notable modification of Egypt's hitherto uncompromis-

ing stand against 'foreign interference' in the future running
of the Canal was prompted by a combination of factors. These,
in ascending order of importance, were, first, economic pressures, second, Indian influence and, third, political pressures
by other Arab states, fearful lest a row over the Canal should
endanger this vital outlet for their oil shipments to Western
markets. The economic pressures imposed by the Western
Powers had largely destroyed the basis of Egypt's triangular
trade with Western Europe and India and the Far East. In the
past this system had been sustained by covering deficits in trade
with the former by credits with the latter and drawing on sterling reserves to bridge any gap. But now, with her sterling
balances frozen, Egypt's trade with Europe had fallen to a mere
fraction of its pre-July figure. Against this, however, she was
able to draw $15,000,000 from her deposits with the Inter-
national Monetary Fund, and a Chinese credit of £1,600,000
in Swiss francs was made available to her in Zürich. India had
also offered to pay for her imports in rupees, while Japan
agreed to accept deferred payment. As for the denial of Canal
dues to Egypt's account, the 35-40 per cent. which Egypt was
now getting, all of which was in transferable currencies, was
enough to tide her over a short period; and, until some major
capital development project had to be paid for, the 'loss' of
60-65 per cent. of the Canal revenues would injure but not
cripple the Egyptian economy.

Of far greater importance were the political pressures which
were being brought to bear on Nasser. The Indians, seeking to
bridge the gulf between their Commonwealth partner, Britain,
and their co-leader of the non-aligned nations, Egypt, were
working hard to persuade Nasser to accept some form of user
participation in the operation of the Canal. Without prejudice
to Egypt's sovereign rights of ownership, they contended that
it should be possible to find a way to associate the Users' Club
in such matters of vital interest as control of passage through
the Canal, the fixing of tolls, maintenance and improvement,
and the settlement of disputes. Krishna Menon, then India's

principal representative at the U.N., travelled ceaselessly between London, Cairo and New York, urging all concerned to
accept a scheme on these lines.

On top of this, while the itinerant Mr. Menon journeyed to
and fro, Egypt's fellow Arab states brought the full weight of
their own influence to bear in Cairo. Angered by Nasser's
failure to consult with the Arab League before he announced
the nationalisation of the Canal, upon which the oil-producing
Arab States depended to ship their products to the markets of
the West, countries like Iraq and Saudi Arabia did not mince
their words in telling Nasser what they thought of his precipitate action. Nor were the oil-rich states the only angry ones.
Jordan complained bitterly that Nasser's move had stimulated
Israel to adopt a more than ever hostile attitude towards her.
In September two savage attacks had been staged by Israel
against Jordanian frontier posts on the pretext of 'retaliation'
for a few minor border incidents for which Jordan had been
held responsible. Added to this, in response to Anglo-French
troop movements in the Eastern Mediterranean, Egypt had
transferred forces from Israel's borders to the Nile Delta and
Port Said, and so had released Israeli forces to concentrate
against Jordan. Therefore, the sooner Nasser agreed to
negotiate a settlement of the Canal dispute, the sooner he
would repair the damage he had done to his fellow Arabs and
to their relations with Egypt.

These were powerful pressures, and their effect in Cairo was
clearly reflected in Fawzi's statement to the Security Council.
For the first time since July 26, Egypt had conceded the principle of user participation in the operation of the Canal. A basis
for negotiation seemed to have been achieved. Certainly Hammarskjöld thought so, and promptly took the initiative of calling the assembled Foreign Ministers of Britain, France and
Egypt to consult with him in the strictest privacy to see if an
agreement could be reached away from the glare of publicity
surrounding the Security Council debates.

Both Lloyd and Fawzi found no difficulty in agreeing to

private talks under Hammarskjöld's chairmanship. Fawzi was clearly under instructions to seek an agreement, provided it did not prejudice Egypt's sovereignty. And Lloyd, although he knew as well as anyone that Eden wanted to force the issue, was himself inclined to seek a peaceful settlement, if one could be found which offered an adequate measure of international, or users', control. But for Pineau the Hammarskjöld initiative was acutely embarrassing. Knowing what he did of the plans which the French Government were discussing with the Israelis, he clearly had to do all in his power to ensure that a state of deadlock persisted. There would be no difficulty about this, so long as he and his British colleague stood firm on the Eighteen-Power proposals, which Nasser had rejected and would refuse to reconsider. But if another proposal were substituted as a basis for negotiation, an altogether different and, for him, more dangerous situation was likely to arise. Fawzi's speech had suggested that, while the Eighteen-Power proposals, as such, were still unacceptable, he would be ready to negotiate on some variant. And if this happened Pineau knew that he would be hard put to it to ensure that continuing state of deadlock which France wanted in order to fulfil her plans with Israel.

As soon as the private talks began, Pineau's fears were confirmed. Fawzi readily accepted Lloyd's Six Principles and showed himself willing to discuss the question of user participation. Pineau now saw that a basis for negotiation was in sight and that he would either have to accept this unpalatable fact and go along with the discussions or renege on everything which he and Mollet, no less than British Ministers, had publicly proclaimed about the need for a just and peaceful settlement. In a desperate throw, he tried to sour the atmosphere and force Fawzi to return to an intransigent line by announcing to the Press that no progress was being made in the talks and that there was no basis for negotiation with Egypt. But Fawzi was not to be put off his stroke by this kind of by-play. And although he felt—as he subsequently told Sir Humphrey Trevelyan, our Ambassador in Cairo—that Pineau was not negotiating in good faith, he continued to treat with the British and French Ministers in an obviously sincere effort to reach an understanding.

With agreement established on the Six Principles, the talks centred largely on the method of giving effect to Fawzi's more detailed proposals about co-operation between the Egyptian Canal Authority and the user nations and about the disposal of the Canal revenues. Fawzi made it clear from the outset that he could not accept the kind of international body to control the Canal that had been suggested in the Eighteen-Power proposals. At the same time he was prepared to look at any suggestions for an 'organised co-operation between the Egyptian Authority and the users'. More important still, he was willing to write into an agreement provision for a measure of control by the users over the allocation of Canal revenues for maintenance and development. He was also prepared to establish the necessary procedures for the settlement of disputes between Egypt and the users, to negotiate the method of fixing tolls and charges and to confirm Egypt's acceptance of all the obligations arising from the Constantinople Convention and of all the rules and regulations hitherto governing the Canal's administration.

In sum, Egypt was now willing to negotiate an agreement which gave the maritime powers substantially all that they were asking. The Suez Canal Users' Association, or its equivalent, would now have a real job of work to do as the organised representative of the users and, without prejudice to Egypt's right of ownership, would be able to safeguard the interests of its members with the full agreement of the Egyptian Government. After two and a half months of bitter exchanges, it seemed that agreement had finally been reached that the Suez Canal would be run as a partnership between Egypt and the users.

Lloyd gladly accepted these major concessions from Fawzi, although he feared that they would come as a most unwelcome development to his chief; and it was decided that a further meeting to spell out the agreement would be called in Geneva on October 29. Twelve days later, on October 24, after further talks with the Egyptian Foreign Minister, Hammarskjöld wrote to Fawzi to prepare the ground for the Geneva meeting by pinning him down to the concessions which he had offered in New York. This letter, of which the text is published in Appendix VI, set out Hammarskjöld's understanding of the new Egyptian position. By the time that Fawzi was able to reply with the considered view of his Government, war had broken out between Israel and Egypt, and Britain and France were threatening to seize the Canal. Nevertheless, on November 2, he replied confirming his concessions and suggesting that negotiations should continue 'along the lines indicated'.

Eden was, of course, by no means happy at this turn of events. In the first place, a negotiated settlement was now in sight which conceded Egypt's sovereignty over the Canal in return for protection for the users' interests. And on top of this, the Eighteen-Power proposals, on which we had insisted ever since the Menzies mission went to Cairo, had been superseded by an arrangement based on Dulles' concept of a Users' Club. Try as I did, I was unable to persuade the Prime Minister that the outcome of Lloyd's discussions seemed to give us the substance of what we needed in the way of guarantees for the efficient running of the Canal. He could only see that our original proposals had been abandoned in favour of a system suggested by Dulles—a fact which filled him with the deepest suspicions. Determined to make one final public stand on our original position, he instructed Lloyd to press to a vote the resolution which he and Pineau had jointly tabled in the Security Council. This resolution, after rehearsing the Six Principles accepted by Fawzi, went on to insist in its operative paragraphs that the Eighteen-Power proposals were the right and proper method of putting these principles into practice. Completely ignoring the concessions offered by Fawzi in the private talks, it also contended that Egypt had 'not yet formulated sufficiently

precise proposals to meet the requirements' of the Six Principles, and invited the Egyptian Government to repair this
omission 'promptly'.

Inevitably this peremptory demand, accompanied as it was
by such a misleading statement of the facts, drew from Fawzi
a curt rejection of the whole of the operative part of the Anglo-
French resolution. And although, when the vote was taken on
October 13 it received the support of nine out of the eleven
members of the Security Council, Russia used her veto and the
resolution was lost.

In Paris there was much relief over this development, which
suited Mollet's plans down to the ground. Fawzi's privately
offered concessions could be conveniently disregarded now
that the Security Council had shown that the original deadlock
still persisted with Egypt, and Russia, firmly ranged against
Britain and France. Besides, the French had been particularly
gratified to observe that Eden was no less keen than they to
overlook Fawzi's suggested compromise and to invite a Russian veto by pressing the Anglo-French resolution to a vote.
For as the Security Council debate came to its inevitable end,
the discussions between the French and Israeli General Staffs
had reached a stage where it had become essential to bring
Britain into the conspiracy.

As I afterwards discovered, when these talks first began, the
Israelis had been reluctant to get involved in French plans for
settling the Suez dispute by force of arms. Although obvious
advantages would accrue to Israel if an Anglo-French *coup de
main* should seize the Canal and force Egypt to grant passage
rights to Israeli ships and cargoes, Israel's Prime Minister,
David Ben Gurion felt that the dispute was primarily an issue
between the Great Powers and Egypt. France might support
him with arms and even with some troops. But the French
were heavily committed in Algeria and there was a grave risk
that Israel would be left in the lurch if she were to launch a
major assault on Egypt with only France to guarantee her.
On the other hand, Ben Gurion contended that the pressures

which Egypt was exerting on Israel from the Gaza Strip and in the Tiran Strait at the entrance to the Gulf of Akaba were becoming intolerable. The Gaza Strip was the main base for the *fedayeen* terrorist raids into Israel, while the Egyptian gun emplacements at Sharm es-Sheikh on the Tiran Strait were preventing Israel from receiving any supplies through her back-door, the port of Elath. And Ben Gurion was more than ready to put an end to these harassments by a short, sharp operation against Gaza and Sharm es-Sheikh. But that was as far as he wished to go.

However, as the discussions progressed, the Israelis gradually succumbed to French solicitations, reinforced by the promise to deliver to Israel no fewer than 100 Super-Sherman tanks, 200 half-track armoured vehicles, 200 trucks and 20 tank-transporters. And by early October, Ben Gurion had agreed to help provide a pretext for the seizure of the Canal by attacking Egypt across the Sinai Peninsula, as well as clearing the Egyptians out of Gaza and the Tiran Strait. French and, it was hoped, British troops would then move in to 'protect' the waterway and occupy the Canal. But there was one important condition to his agreement. The state of Israel had to be guaranteed against retaliatory bombing of Israeli cities by Nasser's Russian-equipped Air Force. This meant an air-strike against Egyptian airfields in conjunction with the Israeli attack. And Mollet knew that, whatever else the French might be able to accomplish on their own, Britain, and only Britain, had bomber bases sufficiently near at hand to take on this essential task.

Thus the time had come to invite Eden to join in the plot. Indeed, it had now become not only necessary but urgent for Mollet to put his cards on the table. For at this very moment developments on the Jordan-Israel border had given rise to a potentially serious conflict of policy between France and Britain, which it was essential to resolve before it should undermine the Anglo-French alliance against Nasser.

9   A Jordanian Digression

At the same time that the talks with Fawzi were proceeding
in New York, the Conservative Party Conference was assem-
bling for is annual meeting in Llandudno in North Wales. The
first item of business to be taken on the opening day, Thursday, October 11, was a debate on the Suez Canal dispute. In
Lloyd's absence at the U.N., the spokesman for the Government who was to wind up the debate was to be Lord Salisbury,
currently Lord President of the Council and Leader of the
House of Lords. Salisbury was a friend of Eden's of long standing; he had been Parliamentary Under-Secretary of State at
the Foreign Office when Eden was Foreign Secretary before
World War II and had resigned with his chief in 1938. When
Eden became Prime Minister in 1955, only the fact that Salisbury sat in the House of Lords had prevented his being appointed Foreign Secretary. And, with Lloyd out of the country,
he was the obvious choice to undertake the task of answering
this important party discussion.

Unfortunately, however, on the morning of the very day
before the Conference was due to start, Salisbury was taken
ill, and early that same afternoon I received a message from
No. 10 instructing me to go to Llandudno and take his place.
Every senior Minister attending the Conference was taken up
with a debate on his own department, and I was the only avail-

able substitute. I telephoned Eden at once saying that, while I would obey orders if there was no alternative, at the same time I would have no time to prepare a speech of my own and to get to Llandudno in time for the debate at 9.30 next morning. 'You won't be making a speech of your own,' Eden replied. 'You will be making Bobbety Salisbury's speech, which has been cleared by the Cabinet. He is sending it round to you by special messenger. Just get on the train and don't argue.' And with a hurried 'Good luck' he hung up.

I realised that I had no alternative. If I refused, I should have had to resign there and then; and however much I might be out of step with Eden personally, I still hoped and prayed that Lloyd's talks in New York might pull off an agreement and so drag the Prime Minister back from the brink of disaster. To resign on the spur of that moment, because I was told to read a speech which would be somewhat more belligerent in tone than anything I would have said for myself, would have been highly irresponsible. So, clutching Salisbury's speech notes, I hastened to catch the train to Llandudno.

One look at the notes confirmed my fear that, despite the delicate situation then obtaining in New York, Salisbury had intended to deliver a very belligerent speech indeed. Not only was Nasser to be accused, once again, of 'an act of seizure and plunder in flagrant breach of the fundamental principle of international conduct', but he was to be threatened with the use of force if the U.N. failed to induce him to satisfy our demands. Before I reached Llandudno, I had managed to tone down some of the more menacing phrases and to make a bow or two to the U.N., by expanding Salisbury's somewhat cursory rehearsal of the respect which we had so far shown to our obligations under the U.N. Charter. But without vitiating the whole speech, I could not make any further changes, and what remained for me to read out was undoubtedly a very combative piece of prose.

Still, it achieved at least one good purpose. It left little, if anything, for the Suez Group to say against the Government and it therefore secured a virtually unanimous vote for the resolution inviting the Conference to support the Government's efforts to get a just and peaceful settlement of the Suez issue. And even though I was not at all happy myself about Eden's thinking, this result was clearly a bonus, for it would scarcely have helped the Foreign Secretary's negotiations in New York for the Conservative Party to have been in a turmoil of disagreement at this stage.

I returned to London on Thursday afternoon to find Eden highly delighted with the way everything had gone at Llandudno, which had set the stage for his traditional solo performance as party leader on the final day of the Conference. As always at such moments, he was full of generous praise, and he did not seem to notice that I had blunted some of Salisbury's sharper barbs. But when I expressed my own relief at the reports which Lloyd was sending about Fawzi's newly negotiable attitude in New York, the old note of acidity returned. Eden would not allow that this changed matters at all. The Egyptians would never stick to any concessions and we must therefore stick to our demands. And if this meant deadlock, then we would have to force the issue somehow before Nasser could consolidate his act of piracy. The French were in complete agreement with this view, never mind the paper contracts in which Fawzi might be seeking to entangle Pineau and Lloyd. And France had shown that she was the only one of our allies who was really concerned to gain a settlement that would do justice to our needs.

However, at the very moment that Eden was emphasising to me the identity of interest between Britain and France, an awkward and explosive situation in the Middle East was threatening to put the two countries on opposite sides of the Arab-Israeli fence. This new threat arose out of a series of so-called 'reprisal' attacks by Israel on Jordan, with whom Britain had a treaty of alliance. Mollet knew that, where Nasser was concerned, he could count on Eden's support for any practicable measures to bring down this 'menace' to British and French interests in the Arab world. But Britain's reactions to Israel's recent assaults on Jordan seemingly threatened to obstruct French plans for creating an Anglo-French-Israeli combination to destroy Nasser.

Britain was at this point very much afraid that King Hussein might feel tempted to turn to Egypt for moral and material support against Israel. After the first of the recent Israeli attacks King Saud had met with Nasser and with Shukri Kuwaitly, the President of Syria, on September 22. The outcome of this gathering of what to Britain were the three most sinister powers in the Arab world was an offer of substantial aid to Jordan, accompanied by suggestions for associating the Jordanian army with the joint Egyptian-Syrian military command, which had been established since October, 1955. Hussein's first response was to make a similar proposal to his Hashemite cousin, King Feisal, for linking the armies of Jordan and Iraq. But the ensuing talks had broken down in disagreement as to whether an Iraqi or Jordanian officer should hold the post of Commander-in-Chief, the Iraqis being unwilling to submit to the authority of General Glubb's young successor, Ali Abu Nuwar, who was still in his thirties.

Then a few days later, on October 10, the Israelis launched their heaviest attack yet on the frontier village of Qalqilya, killing 100 Jordanians. Britain, through the mouth of the Foreign Secretary, issued the strongest condemnation of Israel's action at a meeting of the U.N. Security Council and reminded the Israeli Government of her obligations to Jordan. Hussein at once contacted General Sir Charles Keightley, C.-in-C. British Forces in the Middle East, suggesting that the scope and strength of the Israeli attack presaged something more far-reaching than a reprisal raid and that in the circumstances he might have to invoke the Anglo-Jordanian Defence Treaty. But, despite Lloyd's strong language at the U.N., the British response had been somewhat less than forthcoming, and the King was left in no doubt of Britain's reluctance to become involved in actual hostilities. In desperation, therefore, over his seeming isolation in face of a possible full-scale war with Israel, Hussein then turned to Egypt, and an urgent appeal was sent to Cairo by Jordan's Foreign Minister, Abdul Hadi.

This was more than Eden could tolerate; and with a desperation now almost equalling that of Hussein, he telegraphed to Baghdad, begging Nuri to forestall this incipient defection of our mutual ally into Nasser's camp by offering to send an Iraqi brigade to reinforce Jordan. Such a gesture would not, it was pointed out, raise any problems about the command structure, as these troops could remain fully under Iraqi orders. But it might help to prevent Hussein committing himself irretrievably to a joint-command arrangement under Nasser. As always, Nuri responded to the pleas of his British ally; Hussein accepted the Iraqi offer with much relief; and arrangements were immediately put in hand for the despatch of an Iraqi brigade to Jordan.

However, directly they were informed of this development by the British Charge d'Affaires in Tel Aviv, the Israeli Government protested both publicly and diplomatically in Paris that the projected Iraqi move constituted a hostile threat to Israel. General Moshe Dayan, who was currently Israeli Commander-in-Chief, has since revealed in his *Diary of the Sinai Campaign* that the entry of Iraqi forces into Jordan was one of the three eventualities which could have touched off an Israeli move to capture the west bank of the Jordan River. The French were left in no doubt about this, and they therefore feared that if the Iraqis went ahead, with Britain allied to Jordan and with British troops stationed on Jordanian soil, it would be the end of any hopes of mounting an Anglo-French-Israeli assault on Egypt. For Mollet the possibility of Jordan joining Egypt, if she was not joined by Iraq, held no qualms. Jordan was an Arab state, like Egypt and the others; and as such she was hostile to France and still more to France's new ally, Israel. But, somehow or other, Britain had to be extricated from this present predicament, and the Israelis prevented from indulging in a futile and dangerous digression against Jordan. And the only way to do this was to exert all possible pressure on Eden to stop the Iraqi move.

This the French Government proceeded to do. On the eve of the final deadlocked meeting of the Security Council, the Israeli protest was passed to London, together with a message imploring Eden to restrain the Iraqis. Nothing was said about any Franco-Israeli plans for attacking Egypt. But the point was made that Britain surely did not want to provoke a situation in which she would find herself fighting for Jordan against Israel at a time when all efforts should be concentrated on the reckoning with Nasser.

Eden was much embarrassed by the French plea. Although he did not then know what lay behind it, he was fully alive to the possibilities of Israel launching a preventive war against Jordan and occupying what remained of Arab Palestine, up to the Jordan River. Yet it was, at the same time, imperative to stop Hussein being absorbed by Nasser under the cloak of Egyptian protection. British prestige was once again at stake here. Besides, if Jordan went, Iraq would be dangerously undermined, and Iraq was a vital British asset as an ally in the Baghdad Pact and the site of an essential link in the chain of Britain's air defences of the Middle and Far East.

Caught in two minds, Eden elected to ask Nuri for guarantees that his troops would not be stationed anywhere near the Israeli border so that they might be seen to be playing a purely defensive role. But although Nuri gave this assurance readily enough, it did not satisfy the Israelis, who promptly came back with their original demand that the Iraqi troop movement be called off altogether. Once again Eden temporised, this time asking Nuri to send only a token force of one infantry regiment. And once again Nuri consented.

But the Israelis were not to be mollified either by Eden's compromise or by Nuri's assurances. Ben Gurion was at this stage highly suspicious of Britain and did not know where she stood. Eden was known to be determined to crush Nasser, but his Guildhall speech about the need for adjustment in Israel's frontiers, added to his earlier reputation for sympathy towards the Arab world, had marked him down as an 'enemy' of Israel. In their suspicious way the Israelis had interpreted British support for the projected Iraqi move as heralding an attempt by Britain to force Israel to abandon the Arab territories which she had seized in the 1948-9 Arab-Israeli War and to return to the frontiers laid down in the United Nations Partition Plan of 1947, under which the state of Israel came into being. A few days earlier Nuri had said in an interview with the London *Times* that nothing less than this could bring about an Arab-Israeli settlement. Therefore, the Israelis reasoned, taken together with the Guildhall speech, the British request to Nuri to move troops into Jordan must be the first phase of a plan to impose a major territorial sacrifice on Israel. Or, as Dayan commented in his diary: 'At the very moment when they [the British] are preparing to topple Nasser, who is a common enemy of theirs and Israel's, they insist on getting the Iraqi Army into Jordan, even if such action leads to war between Israel and Jordan in which they, the British, will take part against Israel. The result will be that instead of bringing down Nasser . . . they will leave Nasser gobbling up his prey while they rush off to start a new Israel-Britain-Jordan conflict.'

Needless to say, the Israelis lost no opportunity to make these views well known to the French. And when it became clear to Paris that Eden was reluctant to call off the Iraqi move completely, Mollet decided that the time had come to take his British ally into his confidence and broach the idea of a concerted Anglo-French-Israeli move to seize the Suez Canal. With the Iraqis poised to enter Jordan, there was not a moment to be lost in explaining the situation to Eden and pressing him to stop Nuri moving. Once this had been done and the Israelis could be assured that Britain was to be their full ally in the concerted attack on Egypt, Ben Gurion would probably calm down about Jordan and concentrate on the main objective. Accordingly, on the morning of October 13, Mollet telegraphed to say that two emissaries would be descending on us on the following day with a message of the utmost importance for the Prime Minister. The emissaries were M. Albert Gazier, the Minister of Labour and acting Foreign Minister in Pineau's absence, and General Maurice Challe, Deputy Chief of Staff for the Air Force, who later figured prominently in the Algerian 'Generals' Plot' against President de Gaulle. Their journey was to be in complete secrecy and to this end it was suggested that they should land on the military side of Northolt Airport and then proceed to Chequers rather than Downing Street for their talks.

I immediately telephoned this information to the Prime Minister, who was then at Llandudno preparing to make his speech at the Conference's final rally that afternoon. He agreed to receive his visitors at Chequers and asked me to join him for lunch before they arrived. A moment later Sir Gladwyn Jebb, our Ambassador in Paris, came through on the telephone to say that, while he had been unable to discover what was the purpose of the Gazier-Challe visit, he had just gleaned some very disquieting information about French policy in the Middle East, and that he was hurrying to London to discuss it with me.

In a few hours Jebb arrived. His news was certainly most disquieting. According to information just received, the French Government had recently delivered to Israel no fewer than seventy-five of the latest French Mystère fighter aircraft. In accordance with the established procedures for consultation about arms deliveries between the signatories of the Tripartite Declaration, the French had cleared with us and the Americans the delivery of twelve Mystères several months before. But nothing had been said to us about this further huge consignment and, although the figure reported turned out to be an exaggeration, the fact remained that the French were clearly hoodwinking their Tripartite partners in a deliberate attempt to tip the arms balance in the Middle East in Israel's favour. Coming on top of the recent series of attacks on Jordan, this could only encourage the Israelis to further and more perilous trials of strength with their Arab neighbours.

That evening I telephoned to Eden on his return from Llandudno and told him about the Mystères. He was very worried.
Did I think that this meant that the French were putting the
Israelis up to attack Jordan, he asked? I replied that this was
anyone's guess, but that the experts in the Foreign Office felt
this was a possible explanation, in the light of all the fuss which
Tel Aviv and Paris had recently been making about the movement of Iraqi troops into Jordan. I also took the opportunity
to suggest that perhaps we had done the wrong thing in dis-
couraging Nuri, and that we should now give him the green
light to move into Jordan and to move in strength so as to deter
the Israelis. But Eden was not having this. It was far too dangerous, he said. To bring in the Iraqis might well have the
opposite effect on the Israelis. We had been warned by the
French that such a move might start a shooting war between
Israel and Jordan, which would put us on the 'wrong side' and
opposed to France. How could a few Iraqis deter the Israelis?
Had I not just told him that, with the Mystères, Israel was assured an absolute superiority in the air?

I argued that the Israelis might not want to get involved in a
war with Britain. Besides, what had happened to his earlier
determination to keep Jordan out of a military alliance with
Egypt? But this only served to exacerbate Eden, who brought
the conversation to an end by shouting down the telephone,
'I will not allow you to plunge this country into war merely to
satisfy the anti-Jewish spleen of you people in the Foreign
Office!'

Sunday, October 14, dawned as a glorious autumn day, radiant
with sunshine and crisp as a biscuit. Yet as I drove down to
Chequers I could not suppress a feeling of foreboding about
the forthcoming encounter with Mollet's emissaries. On arrival
I told the Prime Minister that we had just heard that morning from Sir Michael Wright, our Ambassador in Baghdad,
that Nuri had taken our last request reasonably well, but
was puzzled by our sudden concern for Israeli susceptibili-
ties. In view of this reaction, I hoped we would not press him
for any more reassurances for Israel, no matter what our French
visitors might demand of us. Eden smiled and said that from
his knowledge of Nuri he would proceed very cautiously and
would probably not move at all for the next day or so. This
would give us time to discover what the French had to tell us
and to make our plans accordingly.

During lunch I tried to steer the conversation round to the
good work which Lloyd had done with Fawzi at the United
Nations. But Eden was not to be drawn into any comment on
the New York negotiations, and instead spent most of the
lunch-hour talking about his reception by the Party Conference at Llandudno. Then at three o'clock the Frenchmen
arrived and were escorted into the Prime Minister's study, followed by Eden's Private Secretary, and myself.

After the initial courtesies had been disposed of, Gazier opened the discussion with a further appeal that we should halt all Iraqi movements into Jordan. We were playing with fire, he said. The French Government were in much closer touch with Tel Aviv than we were, and they knew that the Israelis were in a highly nervous state about the Iraqis. It would not be safe to write off their threats as mere bluff. Did we really want to risk provoking a situation in which we were on the opposite side to France at a time when our two countries should be at one in every sphere, and most especially in the Middle East?

I jumped in at this point to say that we had already pushed Nuri far enough. We had persuaded him to station his troops in north-east Jordan, to issue strict instructions that they were not to cross to the west bank of the Jordan River or in any way to present the smallest 'threat' to Israel, and finally to send only a token force of battalion strength. We could not now forbid him to move at all. After all, the idea of sending Iraqi troops to reinforce Hussein had sprung from us and not from Nuri. But my arguments were in vain. For Eden, whose antennae had begun to sense that Gazier's appeal might be the prelude to some further and more 'positive' proposal for joint Anglo-French action, cut me short by saying that he would, at any rate, ask Nuri to suspend his move temporarily.

I then passed a note to the Prime Minister suggesting that, having conceded this much to the French, they should now be asked, for their part, to suspend delivery of the Mystères to Israel. But Eden, now all agog to hear what Gazier would have to say next, replied, 'Later.' Gazier then proceeded to ask us what would be Britain's reaction if Israel were to attack Egypt. Eden replied that this was a very difficult question. The Tripartite Declaration would presumably be invoked, and this would involve us as signatories.

'But would you resist Israel by force of arms?' Gazier asked. To this Eden replied with a half-laugh that he could hardly see himself fighting for Colonel Nasser! Then, casting his mind back to the 1954 agreement about the Suez base, he turned to me and said, 'Didn't your agreement say something about our not being obliged to send troops if Egypt was attacked by Israel?'

I replied that the agreement provided that our right to 're-activate' the base would only operate in the event of an attack on Egypt by an outside power and that Israel had been specifically excluded from the interpretation of an 'outside power'. But this provision only governed our rights to return to the base and did not in any way nullify our obligations under the Tripartite Declaration to resist any attack across the armistice borders of Israel and the Arab world. We had reaffirmed these obligations publicly on countless occasions before and since the 1954 agreement had been signed, and there was no getting away from them.

Eden looked somewhat crestfallen at this. But a moment later he could scarcely contain his glee when Gazier reminded him that the Egyptians had recently contended that the Tripartite Declaration did not apply to Egypt, and that Egypt did not admit the right of its signatories to station troops on her territory merely to fulfil the obligations which they had undertaken in a declaration to which Egypt was not a party.

'So that lets us off the hook,' Eden said excitedly. 'We have no obligation, it seems, to stop the Israelis attacking the Egyptians.'

I thought for a moment of arguing the obvious point that our obligations stemmed from the Tripartite Declaration itself and that, whatever Egypt might say, this meant that we had a peace-keeping role to play in the Middle East. But it seemed more important to find out what lay behind the French enquiry. So I asked Gazier what, if any, information he had that Israel was contemplating an attack on Egypt. For a moment or two he did not answer, but sat looking nervously at the Private Secretary, who was busily taking notes in the background. Then, when Eden had told his Secretary to stop, Gazier said that he would like General Challe to speak.

Challe then proceeded to outline what he termed a possible plan of action for Britain and France to gain physical control of the Suez Canal. The plan, as he put it to us, was that Israel should be invited to attack Egypt across the Sinai Peninsula and that France and Britain, having given the Israeli forces enough time to seize all or most of Sinai, should then order 'both sides' to withdraw their forces from the Suez Canal, in order to permit an Anglo-French force to intervene and occupy the Canal on the pretext of saving it from damage by fighting. Thus the two powers would be able to claim to be 'separating the combatants' and 'extinguishing a dangerous fire', while actually seizing control of the entire waterway and of its terminal ports, Port Said and Suez. This would not only restore the running of the Canal to Anglo-French management, but, by putting us physically in control of the terminal ports—a position which Egypt had hitherto always held—it would enable us to supervise all shipping movements through the Canal and so to break the Egyptian blockade of Israel.

Nothing was said at this stage about the timing of these operations, although it was made fairly clear to us that the French wanted as little delay as possible. Likewise, the military plan was not discussed in any detail, Challe merely suggesting that a combined sea-borne and paratroop invasion should suffice— the sea-borne operation to take Port Said and the paratroops to seize Ismailia, headquarters of the Suez Canal administration, and Suez. Nor did either Frenchman say definitely that the Israelis had agreed to play their allotted part. But from what Challe told us it was clear that the French had made at least preliminary soundings with the Israeli Government, and that they had been given enough encouragement to follow up with this enquiry as to our likely attitude.

When Challe had finished his brief exposé, Gazier wound up by asking the Prime Minister to let the French Government know as soon as possible what he thought of the French plan. Doing his best to conceal his excitement, Eden replied non-committally that he would give these suggestions very careful

thought and would convey his reactions to Mollet early that
week, after he had had an opportunity to discuss them with
certain of his colleagues. He concluded by saying that he would
probably send me to Paris on Tuesday with his answer.

On this note the meeting ended and the two Frenchmen
left for Northolt. Not a word had been said about the Mystère
deliveries to Israel and, when I suggested to Eden as the French
men were leaving that he should at least ask whether the story
was true, he brushed me aside, saying that everything had been
superseded by what we had just been told. I knew then that,
no matter what contrary advice he might receive over the next
forty-eight hours, the Prime Minister had already made up his
mind to go along with the French plan. Nuri's caveat was forgotten, and we were to ally ourselves with the Israelis and the
French in an attack on Egypt designed to topple Nasser and to
seize the Suez Canal. Our traditional friendships with the Arab
world were to be discarded; the policy of keeping a balance
in arms deliveries as between Israel and the Arab States was
to be abandoned; indeed, our whole peace-keeping role in the
Middle East was to be changed and we were to take part in a
cynical act of aggression, dressing ourselves for the part as fire-
men or policemen, while making sure that our fire-hoses
spouted petrol and not water and that we belaboured with our
truncheons the assaulted and not the assaulter. And all to gain
for ourselves guarantees for the future operation of the Suez
Canal which had only a day or so before been substantially
gained in Lloyd's negotiations with Fawzi in New York.

In all my political association with Eden, I had never found
so unbridgeable a gulf between us. And as we returned to his
study after saying goodbye to our visitors, I was at a loss to
know how to tackle him. Deciding to play for time, I proposed
that we sleep on the Challe plan, and that on the following day
I should call a meeting of senior Foreign Office officials to discuss it. I also suggested that no decision should be taken until
the Foreign Secretary had returned to London and had been
given time to weigh the French proposition against what he

had achieved in New York. He was not due back until the middle of the week, having agreed to discuss with Hammarskjöld the arrangements for the meeting in Geneva on October 29, which was to spell out the agreement with Fawzi. This was hardly a suitable matter to put in a telegram to New York. Should we not therefore postpone our reply to Mollet until Lloyd could be put properly in the picture?

But Eden would brook no delay. The Foreign Secretary must come home at once if he was to be consulted. And with that he was on the telephone a few moments later telling Lloyd to drop everything and return to London by the next plane. Lloyd objected that he had other commitments, but eventually agreed to return the following evening, arriving in London at midday on Tuesday. Meanwhile, the Private Secretary was told to organise a small meeting of Ministers for Tuesday morning. I was to represent the Foreign Secretary, until he should arrive in person. Meanwhile I was to consult only two Senior Foreign Office officials. My suggestion that at least the Foreign Office Legal Adviser, Sir Gerald Fitzmaurice, should be brought in on a matter which involved taking the law into our own hands met with the flattest of negatives. 'Fitz is the last person I want consulted,' Eden retorted. 'The lawyers are always against our doing anything. For God's sake, keep them out of it. This is a political affair.'

The decks were being cleared for action, and it was plain that, whatever consultations I might hold with the Foreign Office advisers and however strongly they might support me in warning against this venture, the Prime Minister was not going to be gainsaid. Nothing was now to be done which might upset Israel or divert her attention from the main target, Nasser's Egypt. And before I left Chequers, Eden had insisted that Nuri be told not to move any Iraqi troops into Jordan. When I remonstrated that Nuri would be exasperated by all this order and counter-order and would be more suspicious than ever about our motives, he replied, 'Do you want Israel to attack Jordan?' To which I retorted somewhat acidly,

'I thought our policy was to prevent Israel attacking anybody.'

The following day, Monday, October 15, I conferred with the two officials whom I told of the Gazier-Challe visit to Chequers. The more we discussed the French scheme, the less we could see a single argument in favour of going along with this sordid manoeuvre. The French were not even all that interested in the Suez Canal. It was Algeria that concerned them first and foremost, for they were convinced that the Algerians would collapse if Nasser was destroyed. We should not allow ourselves to be inveigled into pulling these French chestnuts out of the fire.

No doubt the Prime Minister would argue that recourse to the U.N., the Menzies negotiations and Dulles' Users' Club had failed to break Nasser, and that the only way to achieve this objective lay in adopting the French plan. But in his negotiations in New York Lloyd appeared to have got from Fawzi effectively all that we needed to safeguard our interests as users of the Canal and, if we were now to join with France and Israel in an attempt to seize the Canal by force, we should risk losing not only these substantial gains but a lot more besides.

Apart from the immorality of the collusion with Israel, the French proposals meant that we should be acting flatly contrary to the Tripartite Declaration by attacking the victim of aggression instead of the aggressor. We should also be in breach of the U.N. Charter, plus the 1954 agreement with Egypt, which allowed us to send troops to the Canal Zone only at the request of the Egyptian Government. And even if we were prepared to ignore every moral issue, our chances of 'getting away with it' were minimal. We should have the Americans against us, especially as they were in the throes of a presidential election. The U.N. would denounce us and we and/or the French would be forced to use the veto for the first time ever in the Security Council in order to block a resolution demanding action to restrain us. The Commonwealth would be divided with the so-called New Commonwealth—India, Pakistan, etc.

—violently opposed to us; and of the old Commonwealth countries Canada could not be relied on to uphold us. The Arab world would, of course, be united against us and, however much it might damage their own interests, there would be widespread sabotage of oil installations and probably a total stop on oil deliveries to Britain and France.

We might never regain our reputation in the Middle East, and our friends, such as Nuri in Iraq, King Idris in Libya and King Hussein in Jordan, together with pro-Western rulers like President Chamoun and King Saud, might be engulfed and overthrown in a violent anti-British and anti-West reaction. Finally, we should confirm the deep-seated suspicion of many Arabs that we had created Israel, not as a home or refuge for suffering and persecuted Jewish humanity, but to serve as a launching platform for a Western re-entry into the Arab world and a military base, organised and financed by Western governments and Western money, to promote Western 'imperialist and colonialist' designs.

Such were the arguments with which I armed myself for the meeting which assembled on the following day at No. 10. It seemed an overwhelming case. Yet for all the good that they did, I might as well have saved my breath.

My only hope now lay with Lloyd. But would he arrive in time? A few moments later he appeared, looking deceptively fresh after his exertions in New York and a sleepless night in the air. Drawing him aside, I told him what was afoot and what advice I had given on behalf of the Foreign Office. His reaction was spontaneous. 'You are right,' he said. 'We must have nothing to do with the French plan.'

But my relief at this emphatic response was very short-lived. For in effect the issue had already been decided, whatever the Foreign Secretary might say or feel.

My last hope of averting catastrophe was slipping away. Nothing could now stop Eden going along with the Challe plan. And to crown everything I was to be the messenger of his acceptance. There was nothing more to be said. All that remained was for me to ask what precisely I should tell the French when I arrived in Paris that afternoon. To this the Prime Minister replied that he had decided to go to Paris himself, accompanied by Lloyd. There could, of course, be no question of his going in secret, as I was to have done; but there was no harm in this, he continued, nor need there be any undue speculation about his journey. On the contrary, there was a lot to be gained by showing that Britain and France were continuing to consult together at the highest level.

I made one last desperate attempt to button-hole Lloyd before he set off for Paris. But in vain; Eden insisted on his staying to lunch at No. 10, and I returned alone to nurse my forebodings at the Foreign Office. I managed to reach Lloyd by telephone before he left for the airport, but he was in no mood to listen to my pleadings. Eden had clearly used the lunch interval to devastating effect, for Lloyd not only seemed prepared to acquiesce in the French plan, but now took the line that his agreement with Fawzi would never hold. He conceded that it would be in Egypt's own best interests to work it, as she would gain both the management of the Canal and the lion's share of the dues. But, echoing Eden, he kept repeating that we could not trust Nasser to honour any commitment.

The next day I sought Lloyd out to enquire what had taken place in Paris. He was evasive at first, saying that the talks had been so secret that only the Prime Ministers and Foreign Secretaries had been present and no record had been made. But under cross-examination, he admitted that Eden had confirmed his whole-hearted endorsement of the French plan and that further consultations would take place in Paris between French and Israeli representatives. He hoped that we would not have to be directly associated with these talks, at any rate at the political level; but he could not rule this out, as there were a number of crucial political as well as military problems involving us which would have to be settled in a very short space of time. Lloyd added that the French had clearly been in cahoots with the Israelis for several weeks.

I have seldom seen a man more confused and unhappy than Lloyd was on this occasion. But, since it was clear that he had lost control of the situation and that he was no more able than I to stop Eden plunging ahead, there was nothing to be gained by further argument. All I could do, and this I did, was to tell him very solemnly that, if we went through with this plan, I would have to resign. This would be a bitter experience for me, but I could not stay in the Government if it meant being a party to this sordid conspiracy. And I hoped that he would tell the Prime Minister of what I had said.

Lloyd gave a nervous laugh and, as was his habit when embarrassed, sought refuge in a facetious joke. 'There's only one worse thing than having a yes-man on one's team, and that's having a no-man like you,' he said.

The Fatal Decision

When Eden and Lloyd left Paris Mollet was able to assure his Israeli partner, David Ben Gurion, that he could depend absolutely on British co-operation in the plan for invading Sinai and capturing the Canal. So confident, in fact, was the mood in Paris after the meeting of October 16 that Mollet and his Ministers now decided to toughen their Algerian policy. Until this moment they had not been certain enough of ultimate victory over the nationalists to go all out in their efforts to crush the rebellion. But now that Nasser was to be destroyed, the order was given to pull no punches and a plan was promptly hatched to capture the leader of the Algerian rebels, Ahmed Ben Bella, by a singular act of treachery.

Ben Bella was currently visiting Rabat at the invitation of the Sultan of Morocco, who, with Premier Bourguiba of Tunisia, was seeking to persuade the National Liberation Front of Algeria to agree to peace talks with the French. These efforts at mediation had earlier received active encouragement from Mollet himself, in token of which the French authorities had earlier given a safe-conduct across Algeria for the aeroplane which was to transport Ben Bella from Rabat to Tunis for the talks with Bourguiba. But Mollet was now no longer interested in discussing peace in Algeria. And when the aeroplane reached Algerian air space it was immediately intercepted by French fighters and forced to land at Algiers Airport. Ben Bella and four of his nationalist associates were then arrested and taken off to prison in France, where they were to remain until Algeria finally won her independence six years later.

By this act of treacherous folly, France not only forfeited the last vestiges of Arab respect in North Africa, but, when her Suez plan failed to destroy Nasser, she served to prolong her own agony in Algeria by isolating the principal spokesman of the nationalists in a Paris prison and thereby denying to the only *interlocuteur valable* the opportunity to negotiate a settlement. From then on it was war to the death in Algeria—and many Frenchmen as well as Algerians were to die in the six bloody years that followed. Egypt increased her assistance to the rebels, and the Moroccans and Tunisians, rebuffed in their efforts to bring about a truce, joined in giving the National Liberation Front all possible aid and protection.

Meanwhile, in London and Paris the Suez plot was thickening. On the morning of Monday, October 22, I asked to see Lloyd, and was told that he was laid low with a bad cold. When I suggested that I should telephone him, his Private Secretary told me he was not taking any calls. I thought it a little odd that Lloyd, who always enjoyed robust health, should be making such a fuss about a minor ailment at such a time as this. Nevertheless, I let it go, saying I would speak to him the next day. Then on the following morning I tried again and was told that Lloyd wanted to see me.

'How's the cold?' I asked as I entered his room.

For a moment he hesitated and then, looking like a schoolboy caught in some mischief, he said, 'Oh! the cold! Yes. Well, I never had one. I went to see Ben Gurion outside Paris.'

Then before I could stutter out any comment, he added, 'And you, my dear Anthony, will no doubt be delighted to hear that it doesn't now look as if the French plan will come off.' He explained this by saying that Ben Gurion had developed grave misgivings. In the first place, he and his military advisers did not like the military plans, which did not provide adequate air cover for the Israelis. He wanted to be assured that we would 'take out' the Egyptian Air Force as soon as Israeli forces began their attack. If there were any delay in doing this, Tel Aviv and other Israeli cities might be obliterated by Nasser's Ilyushin bombers. But, since the essence of the Anglo-French role in the plan was to intervene only after Egypt had refused to withdraw her forces to the west bank of the Canal, we could not undertake to destroy Nasser's Air Force simultaneously with the Israeli invasion of Sinai. There would have to be an interval to allow Egypt time to reject our ultimatum. Secondly, Ben Gurion was reluctant to become involved in the Suez dispute, although he was keen to take some action to crush once and for all the Egyptian *fedayeen* threat to Israel and to remove the Egyptian blockade of the Gulf of Akaba, which prevented Israel bringing supplies to her back door. Finally, he was not convinced that Britain would give him real support and was therefore reluctant to become our stalking-horse. France might show willing, but Britain seemed to be too tied up with the Arab world—Jordan and Iraq especially. The French Ministers had pressed him very hard to fall into line, but he had refused to give any undertakings.

I did not conceal my feelings of relief at this news. But Lloyd brought me up short with a reminder that, whatever now befell the French plan, the Government would still have to decide how to settle the Suez question. Was it to be peace or war?

'And what will be your advice to the colleagues?' I asked, hoping that he might say that, in his view, we should go back to the New York agreement with Fawzi.

But to my consternation he replied, 'I really don't know. I am so confused and exhausted that I honestly have no advice to offer any more. It would really be better to leave it to a group of the colleagues, such as Derry Heathcoat Amory or Patrick Buchan-Hepburn to decide. They are not only fresher, but probably wiser too than I am.'

Looking back on this exchange, I must confess to some regret that I did not show more compassion for a man who was labouring under a terrible load. But at the time all I could think

of was that at all costs we must not cast aside all the work which
Lloyd himself had done to bring about a peaceful settlement.
And so I flung at him that I had never thought that I would
live to hear a British Foreign Secretary make such a confession
at such a crucial moment of decision. More calmly, I asked
when the decision would be made, and was told that the Cabinet would meet the next day.

Meanwhile, a significant development had taken place in the
Middle East, where the Jordanian elections were held on October 21. Although we had stopped Nuri sending any troops
to bolster up King Hussein, as part of its cover plan to suggest
that Israel was contemplating attacking Jordan rather than
Egypt, the Israeli Intelligence Service had circulated a rumour
that Iraqi forces had entered Jordan. This story spread like
wildfire. Taken in conjunction with Britain's well-known interest and influence in Jordan, it was immediately interpreted
as indicating a British plot to influence the outcome of the Jordanian elections and to secure the return of a parliamentary
majority well disposed towards Iraq and Nuri es-Said and opposed to Egypt and Nasser. And when no Iraqi reinforcements
showed up, because we had warned Nuri off, the conclusion
was drawn that Britain had been scared out of making the attempt. The result was inevitable. An overwhelming victory
was won by the pro-Egyptian parties and those groups who
were dedicated to abrogating Jordan's treaty with Britain and
to substituting a military agreement with Egypt and Syria. Two
days later Egyptian and Syrian military missions arrived
in Amman, and on October 25 it was announced that Jordan
had joined the Egyptian-Syrian military command, and was to
place her forces under the overall authority of an Egyptian
Commander-in-Chief.

The timing of this Jordanian move was to be singularly pro-
pitious for Israel and her Western allies. For one thing, it made
the Israeli mobilisation which was due to begin on October 26
appear as a direct riposte to the formation of this Arab alliance.
For another, such 'proof' of the spreading influence of Nasser

in the political and military alignments of the Arab world was now so much grist to Eden's mill. Any damage to British prestige would be only temporary, now that Nasser's Egypt was to be smashed within the next few weeks.

Not that Eden needed much encouragement to plunge ahead with the French plan. For when I saw Lloyd on the evening of October 23 he told me that the Prime Minister was greatly put out about the meeting with Ben Gurion. He wanted to press the French to make another attempt to bring the Israelis into line, and had asked Mollet to send Pineau to London for further talks that same evening. Once again these took place without advisers being present or an official record being taken. But when I spoke to Lloyd the following morning it was clear that Eden's enthusiasm for the French plan had waxed stronger than ever. Pineau had returned to Paris with an assurance that Israel need have no fears of being left in the lurch and that, if she led the way with an attack on Sinai, Britain would lend her fullest support.

That day the Cabinet met in full to take the fateful decision. It proved impossible to get a final conclusion at one session, and the matter was held over until the following day. But this did not prevent the despatch to Paris of a senior Foreign Office official with further assurances for the French to pass on to the Israelis that we were determined to see the French plan carried out and would do all that the Israelis required in the way of air strikes against Egyptian airfields to forestall the bombing of their cities.

These assurances turned the scale, and on Thursday, October 25th, Eden learned that the Israelis had decided finally to play their part in the Sinai campaign. That afternoon the Cabinet came to its final, and for some at least probably unpalatable, decision. When Lloyd returned to the Foreign Office from No. 10, I did not have to ask how it had gone. It showed in his face and, though he made a brave attempt to be light-hearted, I had never seen him more grim-faced and tormented with doubts.

'When is it to happen?' I asked.

'October 29; next Monday,' Lloyd answered. 'Israel will attack through Sinai that evening and the following morning we and the French will issue our ultimatum to her and Egypt to clear the Canal Zone for us to move our troops in. Egypt will, presumably, refuse, and directly she does so we shall start bombing Egyptian airfields.'

This would eliminate Nasser's bomber force and so protect Israel from air attacks and prevent the harassing of the Israeli advance. The Israelis expected to complete the occupation of Sinai within seven to ten days by means of a four-pronged attack. Three prongs, including a parachute drop near Suez itself, were to concentrate on seizing the Canal Zone between Suez and Ismailia and sealing off the Gaza Strip, while the fourth prong plunged southwards to seize Sharm es-Sheikh, the Egyptian fortified position commanding the Tiran Straits at the entrance to the Gulf of Akaba. These plans would give time for the British and French forces to move from their bases in Malta to the seizure of Port Said, from where they would advance south to Suez.

'And now,' Lloyd concluded, 'I must call a meeting to draft the ultimatum which we shall be sending out. You are welcome to stay and help us if you'd like to.'

So this was it. I felt sick to the pit of my stomach. And for once this loquacious politician was almost speechless.

'You seem to have forgotten our talk of last week,' I said. 'Or perhaps you did not take me seriously. But I meant what I said. I cannot stay in the Government if this sordid conspiracy is carried out. You can draft your own ultimatum without me. I will not be a party to your policy any longer. I feel badly enough as it is, knowing what I know and being unable to do anything about it.'

'I have not forgotten what you told me,' Lloyd replied. 'On the contrary, I have talked to Anthony about you. He's very put out, of course, but he doesn't want to lose you, and if you feel you cannot stay at the Foreign Office, he'd be very willing to give you some other department.'

I said that I was sorry, but this would not solve my problem. I wished to stay at the Foreign Office as long as it was possible to prevent this crazy manœuvre being carried out. But if all my efforts failed I could not remain a Minister in the Foreign Office or any other department. Meanwhile, for appearances' sake, I said that I would continue to come to the Foreign Office and, if I could be of any help in dealing with problems other than Suez, I would be glad to do so. With that I left and returned to my office.

There can be few, if any, lonelier moments in a politician's life than the moment of resignation. Suddenly and inevitably, he is bereft of friends, a castaway adrift on a sea of anger and recrimination, an object of distrust, a man who has committed the cardinal crime of disloyalty to the team. So isolated is he that he begins to doubt himself. High ideals begin to fade in a mist of uncertainty. And be becomes torn between loyalty to principle and loyalty to friends and associates. Perhaps it is easier if he feels angry or bitter against his colleagues. But I could call on no such emotional aids. I felt no anger; only sadness that Ministers, and in particular Eden, who had always in the past seemed such a model of integrity in public affairs, should now debase our standards of international behaviour by this disreputable manœuvre.

Yet although I could not call on anger to support my decision and quell my doubts, there was one member of the Cabinet in whom I felt I could confide—Walter Monckton. Despite the difference in our ages—I had been at Cambridge with his son—he and I had become close friends since the formation of the Government in 1951, and I knew of no one who would give me sounder advice. Since he was strongly of the same view as myself, I knew too that he would respect my confidence and would not try to talk me out of going merely for Eden's sake. I therefore hurried across to see him at his room in the House of Commons. I was not disappointed.

'I know how torn you must feel,' Monckton said. 'But really your problem is quite simple. You are Minister of State and our representative at the U.N. General Assembly. You are not Minister of Pensions, with no knowledge of what is afoot and no obligation other than to vote in the division lobby. You know as much, and probably more than, most members of the Cabinet, and with that knowledge you will be called upon, if you stay, to defend in Parliament and at the U.N. the action which the Government is going to take. Can you do it?'

I felt as if a great load had been taken off my back. The issue which had become so tangled through the conflict of loyalties was now simplified. I knew that I could not defend the Government in Parliament or anywhere else. The action which they were about to take would be a breach of the U.N. Charter, of the Tripartite Declaration and of the agreement with Egypt which I had negotiated and signed almost exactly two years before. And on top of everything else, it would be the result of a squalid piece of collusion with Israel which would have to be denied, even though the denial would be as transparent as glass to any thinking person. Therefore, though loyalty to colleagues still tore at my emotions, they no longer pricked my conscience or blurred my judgment. I had no alternative but to resign as from the moment when Britain began operations against Egypt.

Before we parted, Monckton and I discussed at some length what had brought about this nightmarish situation and, in particular, what had happened to transform Eden so completely. He made no bones about his view that Eden was a very sick man. He had always been excitable and temperamental, but in the last few months he had seemed to be on the verge of a breakdown. Monckton said that he would dearly like to resign himself. But, as a member of the Cabinet, his departure at this stage might topple the Government, with incalculable consequences for all concerned. He would, however, get out as soon as he could.

As I wended my way back to the Foreign Office I was seized

with a sudden wild desire to make straight for the American Embassy and there to tell the Ambassador everything I knew in the hope that this would bring Eisenhower to weigh in and prevent us and the French from going ahead. The Americans had already guessed from information coming to them from secret sources that something was afoot between France and Israel, and it would only have needed confirmation to launch the President in a furious attempt to put a stop to these machinations. But as quickly as I thought of it I rejected the idea. I could not take upon myself such a responsibility. However strongly I felt and however much I might be prepared to do to prevent this act of criminal folly, I could not betray my Government's plans even to their closest ally. I had lost my personal battle and I must accept the fact, no matter how much injury I knew must be done to Britain's name as a result. Yet, looking back on that fateful October afternoon, I wish in more ways than one that I had yielded to my first impulse. No one can tell how we should have then ended up; but that we should have lost less than we did in reputation and influence cannot be denied.

The next day I had to travel to Edinburgh to speak at a meeting of the city's United Nations Association. It would have been a difficult speech to make at any time during the long-drawn-out Suez dispute. But knowing what I then knew made it almost impossible. The briefs which the U.N. department in the Foreign Office submitted to me were quite useless. Ignorant of our intentions, the department was inviting me to reaffirm Britain's loyalty to the United Nations and her desire for a peaceful settlement in accordance with the Charter! How could I possibly reaffirm any such thing when I knew we were about to break the Charter? Yet how could I explain to those worthy toilers in the Foreign Office that I could no longer say these things? In the end I spent most of the speech talking about the successes of the Specialised Agencies of the U.N. in fighting disease and in developing the under-developed countries and wound up by declaring my personal belief that

Britain should continue to set an example to the world by keeping faith with the Charter.

Not surprisingly, when the news broke of the British ultimatum to Egypt in the following week, I received a furious letter of protest from the Edinburgh U.N. Association, demanding to know how I could reconcile my assertions with the Government's action and how, if I believed in what I had said, I could remain a member of the Government. Without giving everything away, I could not explain to them that when I addressed their association I had already severed all effective contacts with the Government. But when they read of my resignation a few days later, they were nice enough to write to apologise for impugning my personal integrity and to congratulate me on my stand.

I returned the same night from Edinburgh to what seemed to be the longest week-end of my life. I spent it visiting my two sons at their respective schools. I longed to be able to warn them of my impending resignation. But I could not do so without giving reasons which I could not give. As a result, a brooding silence fell between us, punctuated by occasional moments of artificial gaiety, and the unnatural atmosphere of our meeting that week-end was very hard for them to take. They must have been even more thankful than I when the week-end was over. I have always been the worst of 'actors', finding it almost impossible to conceal my emotions, grave or gay. And perhaps the most difficult part of those nightmarish forty-eight hours that preceded the Israeli attack lay in trying not to show my feelings of impending doom to my family and friends. Inevitably, the Suez issue was a never-ending topic of conversation on which almost everyone had views and advice to offer to one in my position. 'Why don't you do this? Why don't you try that?' friends would say. And all the time I longed to scream at them to shut up because we had decided what to do, and it was lunacy.

From the moment when Eden decided to go along with the Franco-Israeli conspiracy, the most elaborate precautions were taken to preserve absolute secrecy, even to the point of misleading our friends and 'enemies' alike.

As part of our cover plan, and to heighten the impression that Israel was about to attack Jordan, it had been agreed with the French and Israelis that, as and when Israel began to mobilise her forces, feint concentrations should be made near the Jordanian border, after the rumour had been spread by the Israeli Military Intelligence that Iraqi forces had entered Jordan. At this point we were to 'warn' the Israelis that an attack on Jordan would bring into play the Anglo-Jordan Treaty. This, it was felt, would not only put Nasser off his guard, but would enable us to pose as true 'peace-keepers' in the Middle East.

Nobody was kept more completely in the dark than the President of the United States. After Eden's initial confession that he wanted war had provoked Eisenhower to indignant protests, the President was treated as an unreliable ally. The more he warned Eden that American and world opinion would not support him if he appeared to be trying to browbeat a smaller nation into submission, the more determined Eden became to conceal his hand from the Americans. And after the decision to gang up with Israel had been taken, Eisenhower was told nothing at all. When the first reports of Israeli troop movements reached Washington, together with a suggestion that since the October 16 meeting in Paris Britain had become involved with France and Israel, the President sent for our Chargé d'Affaires, (the Ambassador, Sir Roger Makins, being on leave at the time) and expressed his grave anxiety about the possibility of a flare-up. Eisenhower hinted broadly that the State Department suspected that something was brewing between the French and the Israelis. Over the past several days there had been a considerable increase in cypher traffic between Paris and Tel Aviv, and every American enquiry in either capital had been very obviously fobbed off. The usual frank exchanges between the British and French Military Attachés and their American colleague in Tel Aviv had stopped and the United States Government felt suddenly cut off from its allies, as a complete black-out of communications had been imposed. But the President was unable to draw our Chargé d'Affaires, for the simple reason that No. 10, foreseeing that our Embassy in Washington would be under severe cross-examination once the news of Israeli troop concentrations broke, had decided that it would be better that they should know nothing. Nevertheless, American suspicions had been sufficiently aroused for the State Department to issue over the ensuing week-end an injunction to all U.S. citizens whose presence was not essential to clear out of the Middle East.

Even after Israeli forces had actually launched their attack on Egypt, we continued to pull the wool over American eyes. Before ten o'clock on the following morning the United States Ambassador, Winthrop Aldrich, called on Lloyd at the Foreign Office. But he had no more success in eliciting our true intentions than had the President. The Americans were still to be told nothing until after we and the French had delivered our ultimatum. Aldrich was duly fobbed off with a lot of talk about the efforts we had made to restrain Israel from attacking Jordan. And the first that he was to know of our ultimatum to the belligerents was from a news agency report which reached him as he was about to leave his Embassy for the Foreign Office to receive the official text later that afternoon. Meanwhile, Eden sent a message to Eisenhower in which he said not one word about the Anglo-French ultimatum to Egypt and Israel which was to be delivered that day, and spoke only of the dangers which the fighting might bring to the Canal and of the need for decisive action to stop hostilities. He added that instructions were being sent to our representative on the Security Council to join with his American colleague in requesting an immediate Council meeting. The only suggestion that Britain was contemplating further action was contained in the final sentence: 'Experience, however, shows that its [the Security Council's] procedure is unlikely to be either rapid or effective.' And the later telegram, in which Eisenhower was informed of our intentions, was not sent until after the ultimatum had been delivered and its terms publicly announced. Thus Eden made sure that America could not intervene at the last minute to prevent our going ahead.

The excuse given for this extraordinary procedure between allies was that there was no time to consult Washington and that in any case we hesitated to invite the Americans to associate themselves with the Anglo-French ultimatum in view of 'the constitutional and other difficulties' inhibiting the commitment of the United States to action such as we and the French proposed to take—in other words, the need to consult Congress. And on October 31, when replying to criticisms in Parliament that we had not consulted the Americans, Eden insisted that 'the moment the French Government and ourselves had reached conclusions as to what we should do, I authorised the despatch of a full message to the United States explaining our action before even coming to the House.'

But Eisenhower was not to be mollified by these excuses and explanations. He had guessed that 'the moment the French Government and ourselves had reached conclusions as to what we should do' was several days before the Israeli attack on

Sinai. For nearly a week he had suspected that France and Israel, and probably Britain too, were concocting a plan to settle the Suez Canal issue by force. And directly he learned—from the news tapes—of the Anglo-French ultimatum to Egypt and Israel, he knew that all his suspicions had been only too well founded.

He had been duped in an unforgivable way, and both he and his Government colleagues were very angry indeed. So angry were they that, when the Security Council met on the morrow of the Israeli attack, the American delegate, Henry Cabot Lodge, refused to heed the pleas for time made by his British colleague, Sir Pierson Dixon, and insisted on pressing his resolution demanding an Israeli withdrawal to an immediate vote, thus ranging the United States publicly and unequivocally against Britain and France. Nor was this the end of the story. For not only did Lodge subsequently maintain his indignation towards the British delegation, ignoring all our requests for compromise in the debates which followed in the General Assembly, but when Eden and Mollet invited themselves to Washington for talks with Eisenhower, after the fighting had ended in the Canal Zone, they met with an unprecedented rebuff.

13   War

The more the Americans felt cut off from contact with Britain and France, the more frantic became their efforts to maintain the precarious peace in the Middle East. The Israeli Ambassador in Washington was summoned and warned that America would stand by her obligations under the Tripartite Declaration and would oppose whomsoever committed aggression across the armistice frontiers of Israel. He was also told not to act on the assumption that the United States would be divided or immobilised by consideration of the Zionist vote in the forthcoming presidential election. A similar warning was sent on October 28 in a personal message from Eisenhower to Ben Gurion, with the sweetener of an offer to discuss the problem of Israel's security with Britain and France, America's co-signatories of the Tripartite Declaration. And at the same time America's representatives in the capitals of Israel's Arab neighbours were told to urge the need for restraint.

Inevitably, all Eisenhower's urgings were ignored and all his bluffs called by Israel. As General Dayan has explained all too clearly, this was the opportunity to settle accounts with the Arabs for which all Israelis had been waiting. Never before had Israel been promised the military support of two major powers in an attack on Egypt, jointly planned and executed. For Israel this offered the irresistible prospect of destroying the

Egyptian Army and, by occupying the Sinai Peninsula, of neutralising the Arab stranglehold on the Gulf of Akaba and so
forcing a passage for oil-tankers and other ships to bring supplies to the port of Elath. And, however Ben Gurion might wish
to remain outside the Western Powers' dispute with Egypt
over the Canal, Israel could look forward with relish to an
Anglo-French occupation from Port Said to Suez, which would
allow her to use the Canal for her ships and cargoes. So, on the
afternoon of October 29, Israeli forces crossed into Sinai and
began their attack on Egypt.

On the following morning Mollet and Pineau flew to London for the ostensible purpose of discussing the 'grave issues'
posed by the Israeli invasion and drawing up the terms of the
Anglo-French ultimatum to the belligerents. This document,
which had, of course, been prepared five days earlier, began
by calling upon both sides to stop fighting and to withdraw
their forces to a distance of ten miles on each side of the Suez
Canal. And it concluded with the demand addressed solely to
the Egyptians that Anglo-French forces should be allowed to
move 'temporarily' into key positions at Port Said, Ismailia
and Suez. Egypt and Israel were to be given twelve hours to
reply to these demands. And if after the time-limit had expired,
one or both had not undertaken to comply, notice was served
that British and French forces would intervene in whatever
strength might be necessary to seize the Canal and its terminal
ports by force of arms.

The talks with Mollet and Pineau, which began at lunch-
time, finished at 4 p.m. A quarter of an hour later the joint
ultimatum was duly delivered at the Foreign Office to the
Egyptian Ambassador and the Israeli Chargé d'Affairs. The
replies came that evening. Israel of course accepted and at
9 p.m. Nasser and Fawzi sent for Trevelyan to convey
Egypt's refusal. Fawzi has since told me that in all
his diplomatic experience he never saw an ambassador so
shocked and bewildered by his instructions. Ordinarily he
would not have believed that in such an obvious conspiracy

Britain's representative had been kept completely in the dark. But everything about Trevelyan's manner made it crystal clear that he had been taken completely by surprise by the Anglo-French ultimatum and had in no way been privy to the plot which was now being unfolded.

It would be hard to imagine a more miserable spectacle than the meeting of these two men on that occasion. Everything for which they had laboured and the agreement which had emerged from their labours was now to be cast aside in favour of a military decision. Instead of negotiating our way back to a position of control over the international waterway, we were to occupy the Canal and the terminal ports. One act of seizure was to be followed by another and, whether or not it succeeded, relations would be poisoned between Britain and Egypt and the Arab world for generations to come. To make matters even worse, Britain had obviously used Israel as her stalking-horse for this exercise. For if proof were needed of collusion between Britain and the aggressor, it was written plainly enough in the timing of the ultimatum, which demanded that both belligerents withdraw to a distance of ten miles from the Canal at a moment when the Egyptian army was still engaging the Israelis at distances between 75 and 125 miles to the east of the Canal. This meant that, at the moment of its issue, the powers who were pretending to put a stop to the fighting by separating the belligerents were ordering one of them—and the victim of aggression at that—to withdraw up to 135 miles, while the other, who happened to be the aggressor, was told to advance on all fronts between 65 and 115 miles! The burglar, having been caught in the act of breaking and entering, had been told by the two policemen who found him to help himself to half the contents of the safe, while they moved in to take the rest.

At 4.30 that afternoon the terms of the Anglo-French ultimatum to Egypt and Israel were announced to the House of Commons. Seldom in Parliamentary history can there have been a more tendentious pronouncement by a Prime Minister purporting to give the facts of a grave international crisis. To be-

gin with, Eden attributed the entire blame for the recent tension on the Arab-Israeli borders to Egyptian actions—*fedayeen*
raids, threatening speeches, the blockade of the Canal against
Israeli shipping, and the formation of the joint military command between Egypt, Jordan and Syria. He went on to take
credit for the warning given to Israel when reports of Israeli
mobilisation reached London, which had resulted in assurances
that the Israelis would not attack Jordan. And when he came to
report on the Israeli invasion of Sinai, he painted in the most
lurid hues the dangers which the fighting posed for shipping
in the Suez Canal and for the Canal itself.

Not a word did he say about the repeated massive attacks by
Israeli forces on their Arab neighbours, such as the raid on
Qalqilya in Jordan on October 10, which resulted in the
slaughter of defenceless civilians. Nor did he allow any longer
—as he had contended so strongly when Foreign Secretary in
Churchill's Government—that Egypt had a case under Article
10 of the Constantinople Convention to deny the use of the
Canal to Israeli ships. In fact, he saw nothing wrong in anything which Israel had done and attributed the most sinister
motives to every action of the Arab states, and of Egypt in particular, including the most obvious and natural precautions to
guard against the attack which was threatened by the mobilisation of Israel's forces over the last several days. And when
he was asked why Britain had not acted in accordance with the
Tripartite Declaration, he contended that Egypt's attitude to
the declaration had been 'equivocal', and that in any case there
was nothing in the Tripartite Declaration which precluded
Britain from acting as she proposed to do! Later he was to
embroider on this by saying that, since Fawzi had recently
made it clear to our Ambassador that Egypt did not regard the
declaration as giving Britain, France or America any contrac-
tual right to send troops into Egypt, Egypt had forfeited any
right to protection under the terms of the Declaration. In fact,
Fawzi had said no more than all Israel's other Arab neighbours
had contended when, after the Declaration was issued in 1950,

they affirmed that they could not admit any act under its terms 'tending towards encroachment on their sovereignty and independence'. Nor could this alter the fact that, both as Foreign Secretary and as Prime Minister, Eden had on countless occasions unequivocally reaffirmed that Britain was bound by the Tripartite Declaration. In December, 1955, for instance, he had told Parliament that Britain would 'assist Israel if she were attacked or assist an Arab country if she were attacked by Israel'.

Never before had he claimed that Egypt was not covered by this guarantee. Yet now he was trying to twist things so that, instead of going to the aid of the victim of an aggression, we would claim the right to assist the aggressor by attacking his victim. Instead of acting under the terms of the Tripartite Declaration 'to resist any attempt to change the existing armistice frontiers between Israel and the Arab States by force of arms', we were actively encouraging such a change by offering to lend the force of our own arms to that of Israel's.

Later that evening Eden went even further. Ignoring what I had told him at Chequers in front of Gazier and Challe, he insisted that the provision in the 1954 Agreement that we had no automatic right to occupy our Suez base if Israel invaded Egypt could only mean that Egypt did not want the Tripartite Declaration applied to her, if she were attacked by Israel. By inference, he concluded that we were therefore given the right to ignore the declaration in the present case and to take action which would involve not only reoccupying our former base at Ismailia, but seizing 'key positions' at Port Said and Suez as well!

From the very beginning, therefore, the Government's case looked perilously thin. And it was hardly helped when later in the first day's debate Lloyd gave much of the show away with a careless retort to an interruption by Denis Healey. Dealing with the question of who was the aggressor between Israel and Egypt, Healey asked why, when Israel launched the raid on Qalqilya a few weeks earlier, claiming that the action was a reprisal for attacks on her territory stemming from Jordan, the Government had hastened to condemn Israel in the strongest terms. Falling straight into the trap, Lloyd replied that 'the situation between Jordan and Israel is quite different from the situation between Egypt and Israel'. And when this remark was greeted with laughter, he went on to explain himself by saying that Jordan, unlike Egypt, presented no threat to Israel.

Small wonder that the Labour Opposition began almost immediately to smell a rat. For it was rapidly becoming clear that, while strenuously resisting any potential threat to Jordan, whom we were pledged to defend, we had at least tipped the wink to the Israelis that they were welcome to attack Egypt, whom we were determined to humiliate. Somehow Eden's sudden conversion to the Israeli cause did not ring true, and even the most consistent supporters of Zionism in the House thought it very strange that he should now find so much fault with Arab policies towards Israel, and in particular with the refusal to let Israeli ships through the Canal, which he had until very recently accepted as an inevitable, if not justifiable, consequence of the Arab-Israel war.

At this early stage in the parliamentary battle, no Front Bench spokesman for the Opposition had yet mentioned the word 'collusion'. But from the back benches two former Ministers, John Hynd and Christopher Mayhew, were not so reticent. Noticing the emphasis placed by the Prime Minister on the assurances given by Israel that she would not attack Jordan, Hynd suggested that 'we were in discussion with the Israeli authorities about their intention to invade Egypt'. And Mayhew later felt that the Government were 'using this opportunity to fulfil their long-cherished designs to regain control of the Suez Canal ... they are trying to link up the Israeli incursion with the Suez problem'. No reply was made to these suggestions beyond a request by Eden to the Labour leaders not to 'impugn our motives'. And for the most part the debate on this first day was conducted in a relatively quiet and sombre atmosphere, with the main issue turning on the Opposition's plea for an

undertaking by the Government not to carry out the proposed
Anglo-French intervention until the Security Council, which
was then in emergency session, had come to a decision. This
plea was, of course, rejected by Eden and Lloyd, both of whom
made much of the argument that the Security Council was
paralysed by the veto and was prevented from taking the kind
of immediate decisions which were imperative in such crises
as that with which we were now confronted.

Faced with this stubborn refusal, the Labour Opposition
divided the House at the end of the debate. Then, only an
hour after this division had taken place, Britain was herself to
paralyse the Security Council and prevent an immediate decision by casting her veto, together with France, against the
American cease-fire resolution, which was endorsed by seven
of the eleven members of the Security Council. This resolution, which was clearly intended to substitute United Nations
action for Anglo-French intervention, called for an immediate
withdrawal of Israeli forces and called on all U.N. member
states 'to refrain from the use of force or threat of force in the
area' and 'from giving any military, economic or financial assistance to Israel so long as it has not complied with the resolution'. When it failed by reason of the Anglo-French veto, the
Soviet representative moved a resolution in similar terms, only
to meet with the same fate as his American colleague. Again
the resolution was supported by seven out of the eleven Council members, and again it was vetoed by Britain and France.

My warnings to my colleagues about isolating ourselves from
the rest of the world were coming true all too rapidly. First
the Labour party, and now the Americans and the United
Nations had ranged themselves against us. As for the Russians
and the Arab world, the hostility of the latter was a foregone
conclusion and the former, who were currently engaged in the
bloody business of suppressing the rebellion which had just
broken out against Russian rule in Hungary, were only too
anxious to see Britain and France sharing the 'dock' with them
at the United Nations. By the following day the Commonwealth

had joined the ranks of our opponents. India had condemned us and Israel in the strongest terms, Canada had expressed her profound regret at our action, New Zealand had said the same in slightly less frigid terms; and although she and Australia were later to give us their reluctant support in the U.N. General Assembly, the Australian delegation had voted against us in the Security Council.

Of all the many twists and turns that British policy took during the Suez crisis, there were few which affected me more deeply than the casting of our two vetoes in that Security Council debate. Up till that moment we had a record second to none in the United Nations; and I felt a measure of personal pride that, even on such difficult colonial issues as Cyprus, where sometimes no American support was forthcoming to pull the large bloc of Latin American nations into line with us, we had always managed in the end to persuade the majority of member states to accept our word and to trust in our good faith to work out a just and peaceful solution. Now all that was spoiled; and our record bore an ugly stain. We had failed to carry any sort of majority with us, because we were acting against all our traditions and seemed more concerned to offer encouragement and excuses for the aggressor than to join in effective action to stop his aggression. We had done as the Russians had done, no less than seventy-eight times since the U.N. was started, and were themselves about to do yet again, when four days later the Security Council voted to condemn their brutal suppression of the Hungarian rebellion. But, unlike the Russians, we were not going to get away with it, because we were neither ruthless enough nor strong enough to carry our plan through to the bitter end.

14

Uproar at Westminster

The ultimatum to Egypt and Israel having expired in the small hours of October 31, I sent in my letter of resignation to the Prime Minister as soon as I reached the Foreign Office that same morning. Within minutes of its arrival a call came from No. 10 asking me to go and see Eden after lunch in his room at the House of Commons. I do not think I have dreaded an interview more than this one, fearing as I did that he would put pressure on me to stay in the Government, perhaps by switching to another department.

As it turned out, my fears were groundless. Eden's first words were that he knew me too well to try to persuade me to change my mind. Still, it was a painful encounter. I had not seen him since the day when I had deputised for Lloyd at the first Ministerial meeting that considered the French plan. (In those days he had no time for those who did not see eye to eye with him.) And I began by reminding him of what I had said then and added that I was more than ever convinced that his policy was wrong and would lead to disaster. Even if it succeeded, I could not condone our collusion. Apart from the moral aspect, we should convince the entire Arab world that they had been right all along in believing that we had created Israel as a beach-head from which we would one day return to re-establish ourselves in the Middle East. What we were doing now seemed to me to be contrary to everything which he had always stood for—and hence taught me—during his political life.

Eden's only reply to this was that he thought I would be more concerned with the threat to Jordan than with the attack on Egypt. But when I pointed out that the threat to Jordan had been invented by us to cover our tracks, he did not pursue the argument. And as I looked him in the eye, he looked away. Already, I felt, he knew that he was beaten, having tried and failed to act out of character. He was too astute a Parliamentarian not to see the succession of pitfalls before him in the debates that were to ensue in the House of Commons. Even if the military operations were to succeed in Suez, he would have an almost impossible task explaining himself to Parliament and in particular in answering the charge of collusion. And it was almost in desperation that he asked me to agree that my resignation should be kept secret until the Parliamentary storm that was brewing had passed.

I said that, if it would help him at all, I would certainly agree to the announcement being delayed for as long as possible, but I warned him that it might well prove impossible to keep it secret for more than a few days. Already several of my friends and others in Fleet Street were asking why I had not been on the Front Bench during the previous day's debate. They seemed to sense that I was on the point of resignation, and my private secretary had not been able to convince them by replying that I was in bed stricken with asthma. With that we parted, and as we shook hands Eden said with a smile, '*Tout casse sauf l'amitié*. I hope, in spite of all this, that we shall see something of each other in the future.' I have never seen him since that day.

That same afternoon Eden faced the House of Commons, where the temperature was rising visibly in the knowledge that

on the previous evening Britain and France had twice vetoed
attempts by the Security Council to stop the Israeli aggression
in Sinai. To many Conservative as well as Labour Members
this action seemed odd, to say the least, while to some it appeared to be downright sinister. The Foreign Secretary had
been at great pains on the previous day to complain of the in-
effectiveness of the Security Council, due to constant abuse of
the veto. Yet here were the British and French delegates in
the U.N. using that same veto to prevent the Security Council
from ordering a cease-fire in a situation which their own
Governments had proclaimed to be so dangerous to world peace
and to the security of the Suez Canal that they were ready to
move in their own troops to 'separate the combatants'. Could
it be that they had refused to allow the U.N. to order Israel to
withdraw because they wanted Israeli forces to stay in Sinai?
Could it be that they had squashed any U.N. initiative to bring
about a cease-fire because they wanted to use the hostilities as
a pretext to occupy the Canal and its terminal ports? Not only
did the Anglo-French veto suggest that such motives underlay
the two Governments' thinking, but there was also the curious
bias of the ultimatum to the belligerents to be explained. Israel
had been invited to occupy several thousands of square miles
of Egyptian territory from the armistice frontier to within ten
miles of the Canal, whereas Egypt was ordered to abandon
Sinai, to withdraw west of the Canal and to allow British and
French troops to occupy Port Said, Ismailia and Suez.

Small wonder, therefore, that when the House met on October 31 to hear a report from the Prime Minister on the latest
events, it was in an atmosphere of confusion and growing suspicion. But, apart from the scarcely surprising announcement
that Israel had accepted the ultimatum and that Egypt had rejected it the previous evening, Eden had nothing new to say.
Most of his speech was taken up with a justification of Israel's
attack on Egypt as a preventive and punitive measure of self-
defence, which the Security Council should not be allowed to
condemn one-sidedly. (In fact, as Gaitskell later pointed out,

the American resolution did not condemn Israel in terms, but merely called for the withdrawal of her forces from Sinai.) For the rest he insisted that he had been right to refuse the Opposition's demand that the intended Anglo-French intervention on the Canal should be delayed, pending a decision by the Security Council to stop the fighting.

Several times he repeated how essential it was for Britain and France to act rapidly in this situation. Yet when Gaitskell asked whether, in that case, British troops were now in action on Egyptian territory and, if not, when they might be expected to arrive, Eden refused to reply. All he would say, although pressed repeatedly for information, was that he had 'made perfectly plain yesterday that . . . we would take military action at the expiry of the period' of the ultimatum. In the absence of any news from Egypt of Anglo-French troop landings along the Canal, this reticence suggested fairly clearly that, in spite of Egypt's rejection of the ultimatum, no military action had yet been undertaken. And to many members of the House it now seemed that, in this instance at least, the Security Council had in fact acted more 'rapidly' than the British and French Governments. Not unnaturally, this conclusion only increased their suspicion that the Prime Minister and Foreign Secretary were concealing the Government's true intentions from the House.

Consequently, as the debate proceeded accusations of collusion began to multiply. Gaitskell, in a devastating denunciation, said that the Government's action involved 'not only the abandonment but a positive assault upon the three principles which have governed British foreign policy for at any rate the last ten years—solidarity with the Commonwealth, the Anglo-American Alliance and adherence to the Charter of the United Nations'. He went on to assert that the ultimatum constituted 'a transparent excuse to seize the Canal to carry out the policy of force'. And in conclusion he asked the Government to say whether the story currently circulating, that 'the whole business was a matter of collusion between the British and French

Governments and the Government of Israel', was true or
false.

Other Labour members joined in pressing the Government
on this point, including Philip Noel-Baker in his winding-up
speech from the Opposition Front Bench. No longer, therefore, could the Foreign Secretary ignore the question, as he
had done the night before. And, picking his words very carefully, he replied in these terms: 'The Right Hon. Gentleman
asked whether there had been collusion with regard to this
matter. Every time any incident has happened on the frontiers
of Israel and the Arab states we have been accused of being in
collusion with the Israelis about it. That allegation has been
broadcast from Radio Cairo every time. It is quite wrong to
state that Israel was incited to this action by Her Majesty's
Government. There was no prior agreement between us about
it. It is, of course, true that the Israeli mobilisation gave some
advance warning and we urged restraint upon the Israeli
Government and in particular drew attention to the serious
consequences of any attack upon Jordan.'

It would be hard to find in the annals of Parliament a more
disingenuous pronouncement by a Minister of the Crown. Undoubtedly the French were the instigators of the Suez intervention and bore prime responsibility for 'inciting' Israel; but,
to say the least, this was not quite the whole truth. Not only was it
untrue to say that there was no prior agreement between Britain,
France and Israel, but there was a written contract between them
which ensured that there was complete understanding and joint
preparation. And to suggest that in these circumstances we were
innocent of collusion was as unworthy of the man who did it as it
was of the place where it was done.

If any of the Government's critics believed what Lloyd and
Eden told them in the course of this debate, they were in for
a rude awakening on the following morning. For during the
night of October 31—November 1, British aircraft, in fulfilment
of our pledge to Ben Gurion, bombed four Egyptian airfields
—Almaza, Inchass, Abu Sueir and Kabrit—and early the next

morning followed up these raids with attacks on a total of nine Egyptian aerodromes. The bombing was extremely accurate, no civilian targets were hit, and when the raiders had finished their work there was little, if anything, left of Egypt's bomber force. The R.A.F. had kept Eden's promise to the Israelis, who could now continue their advance across Sinai, safe in the knowledge that Nasser could neither retaliate against their cities nor harass their progress in the field.

In England the news of the bombing had a mixed reception. Those who could think of nothing but destroying Nasser and Egypt were elated. But many people were deeply shocked. Even among those who had been prepared to accept the Prime Minister's original statement of October 30 at its face value, grave doubts now began to arise. Nothing had been said in that statement or in the ultimatum about bombing Egyptian airfields. We and the French had been going to intervene to seize Port Said, Ismailia and Suez to separate the combatants, protect the Canal, and stop the war from spreading. But instead of doing this, we were now spreading the war by attacking Egyptian targets near Cairo and other places in no way connected with the Canal.

The reasons for the Prime Minister's reticence in the previous day's debate about the nature and timing of the Anglo-French intervention were becoming all too clear. He could not admit before the event that our next step, far from the police action which he had announced, was to be the destruction of the Egyptian Air Force, and that we and the French would only send in troops to protect the Canal after we had knocked Egypt out as a military power in the air. And the 'rapid' action which could not be delayed pending the Security Council's decision was not, at any rate in the first instance, to be the proclaimed intervention on the Canal by ground forces to separate the combatants, but rather a deliberate act of war designed to cripple Egypt's power to retaliate against her attacker.

The rat that had begun to smell during the first debate on

the Prime Minister's statement was now stinking to high
heaven. And when Anthony Head, as Minister of Defence,
announced the bombing of Egypt in Parliament later that afternoon, the temper of Opposition Members reached boiling-
point. Gaitskell, expressing their feelings of outrage and shame,
immediately demanded an undertaking that the Government
would abide by any decisions reached by a two-thirds majority
of the U.N. Assembly, which was meeting in emergency session at that very moment, and that no further military action
be taken pending the Assembly's decision. Amid a rising crescendo of protests, Head refused to give any such assurance,
and tried to make out that the object of our bombing operations was 'solely ... to induce the Egyptian Government to
accede to the requirements put forward'—in other words, to
our ultimatum. This only served to exacerbate the situation.
Did this mean, Gaitskell and others now demanded, that we
were at war with Egypt? If not, how could any member of our
armed forces who might be shot down or captured claim the
protection of a prisoner of war?

These questions being addressed to the Prime Minister,
Eden then rose to reply. The Opposition, he said, had tabled
a motion of censure on the Government. When this was later
debated, he and his colleagues would deal with all aspects of
the situation. Furious cries of 'Answer. Answer' greeted this
prevarication. And after Eden had tried to contend, with his
Defence Minister, that the bombing was 'in accordance with the
statement we made', general uproar ensued. The Speaker tried
desperately to control it, but, with scores of Members on their
feet hurling accusations and abuse at the Government Front
Bench, he was unable to make himself heard, and was forced
to suspend the sitting for half an hour to allow some calm to
be restored before the debate began on the Opposition censure
motion.

It was a deplorable scene, totally unworthy of the Mother
of Parliaments, with Labour Members booing the Prime
Minister, refusing to acknowledge the Speaker's authority and

rendering any kind of ordered discussion impossible. But as one old Parliamentary hand from the Opposition side later told me, 'We knew something very dirty was going on. But in the face of the Government's denials we couldn't prove it; and so in our frustration we just saw red and all of us completely lost our tempers.' However deplorable the spectacle may have been, the cause was certainly understandable. If Eden had been able to announce that the Anglo-French expedition was on its way to take over the Canal, the uproar might have been avoided. At least he would then have been seen to be acting within the terms of his original statement to the House. But our military plans had been drawn up in such a way as to preclude this. Not only had we promised the Israelis to 'take out' Nasser's Air Force as soon as possible, but the Anglo-French landings were not scheduled to take place until November 6, five days ahead. This was partly to lessen the appearance of collusion, which would have been greatly strengthened if our troops had all been close at hand at the time of the Israeli attack. It was also due to the fact that in the absence of any deep-water port in Cyprus, the sea-borne assault that was to support the air-borne landings had to cross more than 1,000 miles of sea between Malta and Port Said.

The half-hour's suspension seemed to restore a certain amount of calm and the censure debate which followed that afternoon was conducted at a more reasonable temperature. Eden and Rab Butler, who wound up for the Government, dealt at length with the legal situation affecting our fighting services. We had not declared war on Egypt, they asserted, although a state of 'armed conflict' existed between us. British troops were, however, protected by the fact that Egypt, and Israel too, had subscribed to the Geneva Convention governing the treatment of captured personnel and that this convention applied 'to any state of armed conflict'. Eden concluded his speech by saying that he believed the action taken was the only course open to the British and French Governments. 'We stand by it,' he asserted, 'and we will carry it through.'

Yet even as he pronounced these determined phrases, the pressures were beginning to mount which were within less than a week to force us to call a halt and to prepare for our withdrawal.

15

The Odour of Defeat

By the following morning, Friday, November 2, the only good news that the Government had received was of the effects of the bombing attacks on Egyptian airfields and of the progress of their Israeli ally across the Sinai Peninsula. The Egyptian bomber force had been effectively destroyed on the ground, and each of the four prongs of the Israeli attack had thrust deep into Egyptian territory, inflicting heavy losses on Nasser's army, and was well on the way to gaining its objective. For the British and French Governments this had the double advantage of imposing a humiliating defeat on Egypt and of providing a continuing pretext for Anglo-French intervention 'to stop the fighting'. Lloyd was to make much of this pretext in the debate the next day when Gaitskell suggested that the fighting between Egypt and Israel was virtually finished and that no grounds existed any longer for Anglo-French intervention in defiance of the U.N. resolutions.

But aside from this there was little, if any, comfort for Her Majesty's Ministers. And, notwithstanding Eden's brave words to Parliament on the previous day, it was beginning to look doubtful whether he would be able to carry through the proposed Anglo-French action in face of mounting international pressures. Eisenhower had expressed in several messages his unqualified disapproval of the action foreshadowed in our ultimatum and his determined opposition to the use of force to resolve the Suez Canal problem. The United States Government had issued a statement dissociating themselves from the proposed Anglo-French intervention, and making it clear that they had not been consulted by Britain or France. And in the United Nations both Lodge and Dulles were pulling no punches in expressing their sense of outrage over the terms of our ultimatum and the intentions that lay behind it.

Besides, within twenty-four hours of the Security Council finding itself paralysed by the British and French veto, the debate had been transferred on the initiative of the Yugoslav delegation to a special emergency session of the General Assembly. Here the veto did not apply, and all that was required for a valid resolution to be passed was a two-thirds majority. Once again the Americans took the initiative and Dulles moved a resolution which urged 'all parties now involved in hostilities in the area to agree to an immediate cease-fire and halt the movement of military forces and arms', and called on all member states of the U.N. to 'refrain from introducing military goods in the area of hostilities'. After a prolonged and bitter debate, the resolution was voted in the small hours of November 2 by the overwhelming majority of 64 votes to 5, with 6 abstentions. Only Australia and New Zealand had been persuaded to vote with us out of loyalty, and Canada, South Africa, Belgium, the Netherlands and Portugal, together with Laos, agreed to abstain.

So much for the moral damage to our position. But this was not all that we had to face. For as these votes were being cast an even more decisive blow was being struck at us, this time in the material sense. Something had gone wrong with that part of our military planning which provided for the destruction of the blockships which Nasser was known to have assembled against the event of a British and/or French attempt to seize the Canal by force. Not only had we failed to send these ships to the bottom of the sea before they could take up their blocking positions in the Canal, but in one case at least we had actually done Nasser's job for him by sinking a blockship after it had taken up its position. As a result, the very thing that our forthcoming intervention was to prevent had occurred, and the Suez Canal had been blocked, with at least four ships sunk at the Port Said end. Added to this, over the ensuing week-end several pumping-stations on the oil pipeline which crossed Syria on its way from Iraq to Tripoli in Lebanon were sabotaged by engineer units of the Syrian Army. And, finally, in a gesture of Arab solidarity Saudi Arabia had broken diplomatic relations with us and placed an embargo on any shipments of Saudi oil to Britain and France.

The damage done both to the Canal and to the pipelines would take weeks—perhaps months—to repair. Meanwhile, Britain would be forced to make good her losses by importing oil from the dollar areas of North and South America, if she could pay for it. But in the previous two months a run on the pound in the world's financial markets threatened seriously to deplete Britain's dollar reserves. Without credits from the United States, we should therefore be unable to buy the oil we needed; and the Americans were violently opposed to us. Thus all our scheming to get control of the Suez Canal had only led us into an impasse, and there was no alternative but retreat.

Eden had already begun to realise this, both on personal and on political grounds. Sick man that he was, the strain of the last few days of incessant Parliamentary debate was taking its toll of his powers of endurance; for ever since Tuesday the House of Commons had discussed little else but the Suez War, and by midday on Friday the Government was forced to agree to the highly unusual procedure of holding a parliamentary session on Saturday. Besides, unlike the French, he was gravely anxious about the isolation of our position in the U.N. He felt that we could not simply ignore the U.N. Assembly's resolution, even though, as he contended, it did not have the effect of an order, as was the case with a Security Council motion. While I did not see him again after we parted on the previous Wednesday, I know that he felt very deeply the censure which he had brought upon himself from the United States and the Commonwealth. And it was no doubt due to these pangs of conscience that he had, in the course of Thursday's debate, given a broad hint that, if the U.N. would undertake the task of maintaining peace in the area of conflict, he would be delighted to see them do so.

I was soon to learn what lay behind this hint. On Friday morning Lloyd asked me to see him and to help in drawing up a plan for a U.N. force to take over from the British and French forces, which were due to begin their landings on the morning of Tuesday, November 6. The idea was to get Lester Pearson, then Canadian Foreign Minister, to put the plan forward in the U.N. Assembly. Pearson had himself suggested in a speech to the Assembly on the previous evening that a U.N. force should be sent to the area to keep the peace, and had offered to contribute a Canadian contingent for this purpose. The omission of any proposal of this kind from the American resolution was, he explained, why Canada had decided to abstain in the vote. He had thrown us a straw and we were clutching at it in a desperate attempt to extricate ourselves from our predicament.

French thinking at this point was, however, very different from the despondent attitude which now prevailed in London. In fact, the more Eden seemed to be weakening, the more determined Mollet's Government became to speed up the Anglo-French landings in Egypt. Fearing that a renewed demand for Britain and France to cease hostilities would come from the U.N. Assembly on the following Monday, November 5, before the Anglo-French landings were due, they felt strongly that our joint intervention should take place at least simultaneously with the Assembly's Monday session and not twenty-four hours later, as had been planned. Thus, when the demand came, Anglo-French troops would be in occupation at least of Port Said, whereas, if they were still on their way to Egypt, the British Government might find it politically impossible to see the intervention through.

As a first step, an urgent approach was made by the French to the Israelis with the object of advancing the date of the landings by two days and, if necessary, making the initial assault a purely French enterprise. The idea was to capture Port Said with paratroops early on the morning of Sunday, November 4. But to do this with speed and certainty so far in advance of the sea-borne landings required, according to the French view, a simultaneous advance by the Israelis to take Kantara on the east bank of the Canal in order to cover the paratroop drop and to protect the French flank from Egyptian counter-attack. The Israelis, needlesss to say, promptly and enthusiastically supported this plan and even offered the French—and the British too if they wished to participate—the use of any or all of the three approach routes to the Canal across Sinai which were now in Israeli hands. But when the French confided their intentions and the Israelis' concurrence to London, they met with cries of outraged indignation. Not only did our military authorities consider it extremely hazardous to land paratroops as long as forty-eight hours before any sea-borne support would reach them; but, worse still, Ministers felt that it would give the whole show away. The French were told bluntly that it would be impossible to answer the mounting accusations of collusion if the Israelis were now to advance to the Canal itself in a move palpably intended to cover the landing of French troops. How could we then claim to be 'separating the combatants' and 'protecting' the Canal from the warring parties?

Thus this French manœuvre came to nothing, and when Pineau came to London on the afternoon of Friday, November 2, to discuss the terms of a joint Anglo-French reply to the U.N. resolution, he was presented with a still more bitter pill. It was a most unhappy encounter. Gone were the high hopes of only a week before, and when Pineau returned to Paris that evening, it was with the feeling that Britain had already lost much of the determination with which she had entered into the undertaking. True, the air offensive against Egypt was to be continued until the troops landed, and the intervention was to be carried out as planned. True, too, Cairo Radio was still to be silenced by bombing and the dropping of leaflets exhorting the Egyptians to revolt and overthrow Nasser was to continue (although what all this had to do with a police action to separate the combatants nobody bothered to explain!). But the terms of the Anglo-French reply to the United Nations, which Pineau had to accept, spelled unmistakably eventual retreat. The two Governments remained convinced, they said, that 'police action must be carried through urgently to stop the hostilities'. But, having said that, they added that 'they would most willingly stop military action' and give way to a U.N. peace-keeping force if Egypt and Israel accepted such a force, and provided it were kept in being 'until an Arab-Israel peace settlement is reached and until satisfactory arrangements have been agreed in regard to the Suez Canal'. Finally, they demanded that, pending the establishment of a U.N. force, Egypt and Israel should accept 'limited detachments of Anglo-French troops to be stationed between the combatants'.

This was a somewhat miserable mouse to emerge from the mountain of great hopes on which Eden and Mollet had jointly set their hearts less than three weeks earlier. No longer were Britain and France to hold the Suez Canal and its terminal ports until Nasser either fell from power or tamely accepted their terms for the settlement of the Suez Canal dispute. No longer were we to ensure by our physical presence on the Canal that the international waterway was 'divorced from the politics of one power' and that Israeli ships and cargoes should proceed freely between Suez and Port Said. Now we were going to leave all that to the United Nations, and we were going to ask Canada to propose that the United Nations be invited to take over these responsibilities from us. There must have been some heavy hearts in France, and Israel too, when Eden announced the news to Parliament on the following day.

For myself, this dramatic change of policy came as a great relief. But it still did not—and could not—expunge the stain which our collusion with France and Israel had left upon our record. Nor did it make amends for our bombing attacks on Egypt nor cancel the act of aggression which we were still to launch against Port Said and the Canal Zone. Admittedly, we had taken unprecedented precautions to avoid civilian casualties by radio warnings to the local population of impending bombing raids. But we were still in breach not only of the U.N. Charter, but also of the Tripartite Declaration and the Anglo-Egyptian Agreement of 1954, which I had personally negotiated and signed. And, however relieved I might feel that we were now proposing to hand over to the U.N., I still could not defend what we had done and were about to do by way of intervention. I therefore could not withdraw my resignation. And although first Rab Butler sought to get me to do so, and then one of Eden's Private Secretaries called on me on Saturday morning to suggest that I should change places with Jack Maclay, then Minister of State at the Colonial Office, I had to refuse their pleas.

Meanwhile, the Press had become more than ever curious about my continued absence from the House of Commons during the incessant debates on the crisis, and they were now demanding an answer, Yes or No, to the question whether or not I had resigned. It was therefore impossible to stall them any longer and, after discussing matters with Eden through Lloyd, it was agreed to publish my letter of resignation at midnight on Saturday.

Before I left the Foreign Office for good, I felt that I owed it to my three junior ministerial colleagues to explain my reasons for resigning. All three—Lord Reading, my co-Minister of State, Douglas Dodds-Parker and John Hope, the Joint Parliamentary Under-Secretaries of State—were deeply shocked and angry at having been kept in the dark about actions and decisions which, as Ministers, they could be called upon to defend in Parliament. For a moment, they seemed to be on the point of walking out with me. But, after a lengthy discussion we agreed that if all four of us were to resign en bloc, the Government might be irreparably damaged at a moment of

national crisis, and we could none of us want to create a state
of political chaos at this critical juncture. My colleagues were
all somewhat churlishly rewarded for their loyalty. Hope was
promptly demoted and transferred to another department, and
when Macmillan took over the premiership from Eden two
months later, Reading and Dodds-Parker were curtly dismissed from office altogether.

My ministerial colleagues were not, however, the only angry
men in the Foreign Office at this time. The word had by now
got around that I had resigned; and as soon as I returned from
Reading's room I found myself bearded by several senior
officials who had guessed the truth about the Anglo-French
intervention and who felt deeply in their hearts that they could
no longer serve a Government which had so debased our name
and fame in the eyes of the world. In all my five years as a
Foreign Office Minister I had never seen such a demonstration of real indignation from officials normally the epitome of
unruffled calm. And it took a lot of argument to persuade them
that they would be wrong to resign. I reminded them that they
were not publicly answerable for the Government's policy,
as I would have been, if I had stayed in office, and that, if they
were to quit when the Prime Minister was beginning to have
second thoughts about the whole operation, it would be harder
than ever to pick up the pieces and clear up the mess. This
turned the scale, and all of them agreed, albeit reluctantly, to
stay.

These awkward encounters over, I stayed for a few minutes
longer brooding in my office upon the tragedy which had so
suddenly engulfed us all. I hope that I shall never know a sadder
moment than the last quarter of an hour before I left the
Foreign Office for good. It was not only that everything I had
personally striven for in the way of a new relationship of confidence with the Arab world had been undone. Worse than
this, all Eden's—and Lloyd's—own efforts had been nullified,
and every principle for which Eden had stood and fought as
Foreign Secretary had been trampled in the mire. How could

we retrieve all that we had lost in this mad, imperialist gamble? How could we regain the trust that we had shattered and the moral leadership that we had forfeited? We, the champions of the rule of law, had applied the law of the jungle; and with the Russians doing the same, only far more ruthlessly, in Hungary at that self-same moment, the outlook for the world looked black indeed. And then, as these sombre thoughts bore in upon me, a strange thing happened. Outside in the approaching dusk, a storm was gathering. Inky clouds chased by a gale-force wind covered the sky, blotting out the sun and casting a dark and ominous shadow across the scene. In the fading light I looked across my room and saw the dim outline of Sir Edward Grey's portrait and I thought of his famous remark as he gazed from the Foreign Office windows when World War I was declared. Once again, it seemed, 'the lights were going out', but this time not only in Europe. Then suddenly the black clouds parted for a split second and a shaft of sunlight, momentarily released, caught as in a spotlight the globe which stood by the window. For a moment this microcosm of a divided, frightened world was transfused with light in the surrounding darkness. It seemed like an omen.

16

Cease-fire

The news of the British change of heart which Pineau reported to his colleagues on his return to Paris caused such misgivings as to cast doubt on whether we now intended to go through with the planned intervention. And on the following day, Sunday, November 4, the French Foreign Minister was sent back to London, together with the French Minister of Defence, M. Bourges-Manoury, to press once more for an acceleration of the Anglo-French landings. This had been made more urgent than ever by an announcement of the Israeli delegate during the previous day's session of the U.N. Assembly that Israel would agree to an immediate cease-fire provided that Egypt did likewise. This had caused a state of panic in Paris and in London, where it was felt that the Israeli statement threatened to remove the main pretext for the Anglo-French intervention. Urgent representations had followed in Tel Aviv, asking that the Israeli delegate in New York be instructed to retract his offer or at least to hedge it around with qualifications which Egypt would find it difficult to accept. But although the Israelis had complied with this request, it had become evident by Sunday morning that the fighting between Egypt and Israel could not last much longer. The Israelis had attained all their objectives and had taken up their 'appointed' positions ten miles east of the Suez Canal along almost its entire length. The

Egyptians had for their part withdrawn all that remained of their forces in Sinai to the west bank, and they too had offered a cease-fire on the previous day, November 3. Therefore it was imperative for the Anglo-French force to land within the next twenty-four hours if its declared pretext of separating the combatants was to be in any way valid at the time of its arrival.

In the light of these new developments, the British Government duly agreed that the advance-guard of the Anglo-French force, a combined paratroop unit, would commence their drop on Port Said in the early hours of the following morning. Thereafter it was planned to advance on Ismailia and Suez, which General Keightley, the Allied C.-in-C., estimated should be captured by November 8 and 12 respectively.

Thus as the first week of the Suez War drew to its close, British policy had become a tissue of contradictions and Britain's leaders seemed to be torn in all directions. Even as these military decisions were being taken, Lester Pearson, at Eden's request, was tabling in the U.N. Assembly two resolutions—the first to seek agreement in principle on the establishment of a U.N. emergency force 'to secure and supervise the cessation of hostilities', and the second to set up such a force and appoint as its commander, General Burns, the Chief of Staff of the U.N. Truce Supervision Organisation in the Middle East. These two resolutions were carried by 57 votes to none. Yet Britain, poised painfully on the horns of her self-made dilemma, abstained from voting in favour of the product of her own initiative, although she afterwards joined with France in informing Hammarskjöld that she welcomed 'the idea which seemed to underlie' the Canadian proposal!

Even the twenty-four-hour acceleration of the landings did nothing to resolve the contradictions of the Anglo-French position. For on November 4, Egypt, having accepted the first Canadian resolution in the early hours of the morning, repeated her offer of a cease-fire and, by that evening, contact between the combatants had been broken off. And on the next morning, November 5, the Israeli Government informed the U.N. that all fighting had ceased between Israeli and Egyptian forces on land, sea and in the air. In effect, therefore, after less than a week of fighting, and without any intervention on the ground by British or French forces, the position of the two sides were precisely that which the Anglo-French ultimatum had demanded that they should adopt on each bank of the Canal.

Yet as this news was being flashed to New York, British and French paratroops were being dropped on Port Said to 'separate' the already separated combatants and to 'stop' the already stopped war. Within minutes of their descent, fierce fighting had broken out again as the Egyptian defenders sought to hold their city against this new invasion. Hostilities continued until the afternoon, when, after a number of reinforcing drops of heavy equipment had been made, the Anglo-French paratroops gained the upper hand. And at 3.30 p.m. the local Egyptian commander agreed to a cease-fire to allow for negotiation of terms for the surrender of Port Said.

In the House of Commons the Foreign Secretary sought to defend our intervention on the grounds that we could not 'ensure that the Israelis withdraw from Egyptian territory until we are physically in the area to keep the peace'. He also claimed that we were there 'to remove obstructions and restore navigation through the Suez Canal and to promote a settlement of the problems of the area'. And, ignoring that it was on his initiative that Canada had proposed a U.N. force, he sought to contend that none of these ends could be achieved by the Canadian resolutions, and that only the physical presence of British and French forces could 'give the necessary guarantees and prevent a repetition of the events of the past few years'. But this double-talk only served to confirm the suspicions of his Parliamentary critics that the Government's real purpose was to seize control of the Canal and impose a settlement on Nasser. Amid a crescendo of angry protests from the Opposition, he was subjected to one of the toughest cross-examinations ever endured by a Minister of the Crown. If our purpose was to keep the peace and police the area, then why, he was asked, were we dropping leaflets threatening to bomb Egyptian villages and telling the Egyptian populance that they had 'committed a sin' by placing their 'confidence in Abdel Nasser and believing his lies'? And why, if our real intention was not to impose our will in the Suez Canal dispute, did we make our withdrawal conditional on the U.N. not only taking over our police role, but also settling the future of the Canal?

For obvious reasons, no real answers were forthcoming to these questions. And when the Prime Minister intervened to announce that a flash signal had been received from General Keightley saying that a cease-fire had been ordered, the Conservative benches erupted with deafening cheers, and Lloyd resumed his seat looking for all the world like a heavily out-pointed boxer who had been saved by the bell.

But such relief was very short-lived. Within hours of Eden's statement the Governor of Port Said announced that he could not accept our surrender terms and must resume hostilities. On the following morning the seaborne assault force of Royal Marine and French Commandos landed at Port Said and Port Fuad. Fierce fighting continued all day, resulting in heavy civilian casualties and damage to the city of Port Said. And only after further frenzied efforts had been made by Hammarskjöld to bring home to us and the French that Israel and Egypt had stopped fighting each other was a cease-fire finally ordered for the British and French forces at midnight on November 6.

What prompted the Egyptians to resume fighting on Monday evening may never be conclusively established. Perhaps the local Egyptian commander acted prematurely in a well-intentioned attempt to save further loss of life. Perhaps the Egyptians suddenly arranged with themselves that they could count on Russian support in resisting the Anglo-French invasion. If so, they were badly misled. True, the Russians had chosen this moment to fish in troubled waters by sending, and at the same time publishing to the world, notes to Britain, France and Israel threatening to crush the aggressors and restore peace in the Middle East, and alluding darkly to the power of Russia's atomic rocket arsenal and to the possibility of Russian 'volunteers' being sent to help Egypt. True, too, they sought to make common cause with the Americans, suggesting in a note to Eisenhower that Russian warships should co-operate with the U.S. Sixth Fleet to bring hostilities in the Middle East to an end, and proposing in the Security Council that a joint Russian-American military force should intervene if the Anglo-French troops did not halt their advance within twelve hours. But the purpose of all this sudden Russian activity was little more than an effort to divert attention from the brutalities which they were currently committing in Hungary. True to its traditions, the Soviet Union was determined to crush the Hungarian uprising, which threatened the whole basis of the *cordon sanitaire* with which the Russians had sealed off their European frontiers since 1945. Equally, the Russians had no intention of seriously embroiling themselves in a war beyond their own frontiers. But the maintenance of the vital Hungarian link in the chain of Russian national security was costing them heavily in terms of world condemnation. And what better diversion could there be than to join in the hunt against Britain and France over the Suez crisis?

By this action the Russians were also able to pose as champions of the Arabs and to gain credence throughout the Middle East for their claim to have stopped the Anglo-French aggression against Egypt. But although these Russian threats and gestures closely preceded the final cease-fire at midnight on November 6, it is fair to say that they had no more influence on the decision of Britain and France to stop fighting than had our intervention in Egypt upon the Russian decision to crush the Hungarian revolt at all costs. Far more decisive were the political and economic pressures that were building up almost hourly upon the British and French Governments—the closing of the Canal and stoppage of Middle East oil shipments, the run on the pound, the fury of the Americans and the hostility of the Commonwealth, to which was now added a mounting chorus of condemnation from the British Press, including news-

papers like *The Times*, which had earlier supported the Eden
policy without qualification. As Eden has himself recorded, 'we
were being continually pressed to accept a United Nations
Command in the Suez area as meeting all our conditions for a
cease-fire'. And although by the evening of November 6 we
had occupied only one of the three key areas listed in our ultimatum—Port Said—and advanced no more than half-way to
Ismailia, these pressures had become so menacing that we were
forced to abandon the rest of the operation less than forty-
eight hours after we had started it.

To say the least, it was an extraordinary situation. For, in
truth, we had achieved none of the objectives, whether pre-
tended or real, with which we had set out upon this sorry adventure. We had not separated the combatants; they had
separated themselves. We had not protected the Canal; it was
blocked. We had not safeguarded British lives and property,
but had subjected them to the gravest hazards. Nor had we
achieved our real aim of seizing control of the Canal. Least of all
had we toppled Nasser from his throne. In fact, we had fallen
between every stool, and now, not unexpectedly perhaps, even
the French, taking the view that the Americans were bluffing,
turned against us in bitter recrimination for calling a halt when
in their opinion victory was in sight. In the Hôtel Matignon
and the Quai d'Orsay there were murmurings of the old accusation of '*Perfide Albion*'. Once again we were 'a nation of
shopkeepers' who in the final analysis would jettison everything, including national prestige or engagements to an ally, if
commercial or financial interests were threatened.

Certainly there could hardly have been a greater threat to
Britain's commercial and financial interests than that which now
presented itself. Speculation against sterling had been mounting since September, and by November the run on the pound
had developed to critical proportions. In September and October our reserves fell by \$141 million and in November they
were to fall by \$279 million, virtually double the amount for
the previous two months. Nobody had been better placed to

observe this perilous trend than Harold Macmillan, the Chancellor of the Exchequer. Having led the pack in supporting the Anglo-French-Israeli conspiracy, Macmillan now became the first to sound the retreat. On November 6, he had gone to tell Lloyd the grim facts of our financial position. To keep the wheels of industry turning, we would have to import oil from dollar sources until the Canal had been cleared and the pipelines repaired. With our dwindling reserves, we did not have the dollars to pay for it, unless America agreed to help to tide us over with a credit. And unless and until we halted our advance south of Port Said, the Americans would never agree to help us.

It was an irresistible argument and, as Eden has related, coupled with the fact that Egypt and Israel had both ceased fire and accepted the U.N. Emergency Force, the Cabinet agreed that a halt had to be called, although he and several other Ministers did so only with the greatest reluctance. But, unfortunately for them, a mere cease-fire was not enough to appease the Americans. Having bitterly opposed Britain and France for sending troops into the area, the United States Government now insisted that, before there could be any discussion of dollar credits, the Anglo-French forces must be withdrawn or, at least, be seen to be withdrawing.

To Eden this demand came as a bitter blow. Britain and France might have failed in their intention to seize the Canal; but at least they held 'a gage', as Eden put it, in Port Said, and they were currently reinforcing this gage to the extent of some 22,000 troops. Now they were being told to surrender even this small advantage as the price of dollar aid from America.

Not all the pressure for an immediate Anglo-French withdrawal came from the United States and the U.N. Our allies in the Baghdad Pact—Iraq, Turkey, Iran and Pakistan—at a meeting held on November 7, from which the British representative was deliberately excluded, passed a resolution demanding that British and French forces should leave Egyptian territory forthwith. The new Jordanian Parliament went a stage further by acclaiming Russia as the Arabs' saviour whose timely threats had forced Britain and France to call a halt to their aggression. And a few weeks later the Jordanian Government renounced the Anglo-Jordan Treaty. Meanwhile, the Opposition in the House of Commons, in a continuing series of almost daily debates on the Middle East crisis, were keeping up a relentless pressure on the Government to withdraw from Egypt in response to U.N. demands.

The Prime Minister was reminded of his assurance of October 30 that British troops would be withdrawn 'once the present hostilities cease'. But he and his colleagues now retorted that we could not withdraw until the U.N. Emergency Force was in a position to prevent a fresh outbreak of hostilities between Egypt and Israel—a feeble argument, considering that our own forces were themselves in no position to prevent such an outbreak at any point along the Canal, except in and around Port Said. Desperately playing for time, Ministers now sought refuge in the claim that their intervention had been instrumental in bringing a U.N. force into existence, and in injecting new strength and purpose into the U.N., which contention Denis Healey contemptuously dismissed as being 'like Al Capone taking credit for improving the efficiency of the Chicago police'.

More dramatic still, Peter Thorneycroft, the President of the Board of Trade, asserted that our action had laid bare a plot by Russia to take over the Middle East, using Nasser as her instrument. Nasser, he proclaimed, had declared 'the extermination of the state of Israel' to be her purpose and Egypt had been armed to the teeth by Russia. Apparently he forgot that Russia's arms deliveries to Egypt had been common knowledge for over a year, and that well within that period the Prime Minister had himself told the House of Commons that 'Israel is not in my belief at a military disadvantage today in relation to any Arab state or indeed to any combination of Arab States who are on her frontier'. Still more unfortunately for

the Government's case, Thorneycroft's argument was tor-
pedoed two weeks later by himself and the Minister of Defence
in answers to questions about arms deliveries to the Middle
East and about Egyptian war material captured by the Anglo-
French forces. Head's reply showed quite clearly that the
amount of captured war material of British origin was four
times greater than that of Russian or Czech origin. And
Thorneycroft revealed that over the first six months of 1956
the ratio of arms deliveries from Britain to Egypt and Israel
in terms of money value had been 4 : 1 in the case of arms
and explosives and 50 : 1 in the case of aircraft and parts. Over
the five previous years these ratios had been respectively
$2\frac{1}{2}$: 1 and $3\frac{1}{2}$: 1. Who then had been 'arming Egypt to the
teeth' and building her up to threaten Israel? And even if the
Russians had been supplying the vast quantities of arms to
Nasser which was now alleged, why had the British Government continued with their deliveries as if nothing had happened? And why had they, in the last six months, increased
the ratio in favour of Egypt by nearly double for arms and
explosives and by fourteen times in the case of aircraft?

There was no answer to these questions. And, not unexpectedly, Thorneycroft's red herring made no impression on that
growing body of M.P.s who felt that Head had come much
nearer to the real truth when he had told the House of Commons on November 8, 'the Canal cannot and must not be solely
the concern of the Egyptian Government. That is what all this
has been about.' He later explained this curious statement by
saying that it referred not to our intervention, but to the question of clearing the Canal. But no sooner had he done so than
Harold Macmillan was to offer yet another explanation which
flatly contradicted everything that had earlier been said.
Answering a debate on the economic consequences of our intervention on November 12, in which he had been accused
of failing in his duty as Chancellor of the Exchequer by allow-
ing the operations to go forward, he said: 'All my interests
would have been to follow what we used to call a policy of

appeasement. Why have I not followed that? I will tell the House frankly and sincerely. It is because I have seen it all happen before. That was what the Leader of the Opposition thought. That is what he meant when he spoke of standing up to Mussolini and Hitler.' Separating the combatants, protecting the Canal, safeguarding British life and property, shipping and oil supplies—all these arguments had now been discarded. And the Chancellor was now in fact admitting that we had invaded Egypt to cut down Nasser, the 'new Hitler'.

Small wonder that the House of Commons and the country was baffled and confused by all these contradictory explanations and excuses. And as the confusion spread, cracks began to show in the monolithic unity of the Conservative Party. Edward Boyle had resigned four days after my own letter of resignation was published; and men like Nigel Nicolson, Jakey Astor, Alec Spearman, Lionel Heald, Robert Boothby and Frank Medlicott were confessing themselves in open revolt against the Government, while members of the Suez Group, such as Julian Amery, were up in arms because we had agreed to a cease-fire before the operations were completed. It took all the efforts of the Government Whips, together with fervent appeals for unity from Rab Butler and Harold Macmillan, to prevent the Party from being split from top to bottom. Still, thanks to these efforts and to that inherent sense of self-preservation which holds the Conservative Party together in moments of crisis, the Government were able to command a comfortable majority whenever the House divided on the Suez issue.

Not so easy was their problem in trying to buy time with the Americans, who alone held the key to the economic prison into which we had landed ourselves and who, even after the presidential election had given Eisenhower a landslide victory, were proving themselves highly uncompromising gaolers. In vain Eden tried to dissuade them from insisting on our withdrawal before any talks about credits could be held. In a personal telephone conversation with Eisenhower he fell back on the Rus-

sian bogy. If we withdrew immediately from Port Said, he said,
the Russians would simply carry on from where they had been
interrupted by our intervention. For a moment this introduc-
tion of the Communist spectre seemed to have done the trick.
And when Eden invited himself and Mollet to Washington for
an immediate discussion of the situation, Eisenhower was personally inclined to agree. But, after further consultation with
his advisers, he reversed his gears and demanded that Britain
and France must accept withdrawal from Egypt before
any meeting could take place between the three heads of
Government.

A prolonged wrangle now ensued between the Americans
and ourselves. Eden insisted that British and French forces
could not pull out until the U.N. Emergency Force had established itself in the area. Besides, he contended that we must be
given time to clear the Canal. Our forces had brought with them
the necessary equipment for raising and removing the forty-
seven Egyptian blockships now sunk in the Canal, and they
should be allowed time and opportunity to tackle this task at
least at the Port Said end. But the United States Government
was in no mood to compromise on their stand. And although,
to sugar the pill, we offered to place our salvage teams under
U.N. control, Hammarskjöld, backed by yet another massive
General Assembly vote for immediate Anglo-French withdrawal, informed us that no arrangements could be made to
clear the Canal or settle its future administration until we had
removed our troops.

Lloyd flew to America a week after the cease-fire to try to
work out some compromise. But the Americans proved to be
unbending, and Hammarskjöld, after himself paying a flying
visit to Cairo, was more than ever insistent that the Anglo-
French troops must be withdrawn. The longer they stayed in
Port Said the greater became the risk of civic riots and of re-
prisals against British and French nationals in Egypt. One of
the most astonishing features of the whole crisis had been the
way in which the Egyptian police had been able to carry out

Nasser's undertaking to Trevelyan, after our ultimatum had been presented, that British lives and property would be protected. But there was a limit to what the authorities could do in such a situation, especially when tales of Egyptian casualties in the Port Said fighting were losing nothing in the telling in the cafés of Cairo and Alexandria. After all, we had bombed and blasted our way into the country and were now occupying one of its leading cities.

Thus in ten days of argument in New York all that Lloyd was able to achieve was to deny Egypt a veto on the composition and ultimate location of the U.N. force and the duration of its stay in the Middle East. His attempts to secure the inclusion of British and French contingents foundered on the argument that, if any of the Great Powers were included, it would be impossible to deny Russia a part in the force—a prospect which sent cold shivers down the spine of every member of Eden's Cabinet, let alone of Eisenhower's. And when Lloyd reported these meagre results to London, the writing on the wall spelled 'Withdrawal' in clear and unmistakable letters for Eden and his colleagues. Petrol-rationing had been announced in Britain and France and, until the Canal was cleared, we would be dependent on America for help in buying the oil essential for our industry. Even if we could clear Port Said's harbour before our oil reserves ran out, we could not remove the blockships in other parts of the Canal without Egyptian co-operation. And Egyptian co-operation, like American aid, would not be forthcoming until we were seen to be withdrawing.

Yet even at this stage Eden refused to give the order for more than a token withdrawal of one British infantry battalion in response to the arrival in Port Said of an advance party of the U.N. force on November 21. Officially it was said that we could not do more until the U.N. had shown whether they could carry out the responsibilities which they had assumed. More likely, it was that the French insisted that we should stay. Because of their commitments in Algeria, they had themselves withdrawn the equivalent of about three battalions—one-third of their force of 8,500 men. But they were still arguing that we should call the Americans' bluff and stand firm against an early withdrawal of all our forces. Eisenhower, they insisted, would never dare to allow our industries to be paralysed for lack of dollar credits to buy the essential supplies of oil.

17

Retreat

For all Eden's last-minute resistance, the end was not far off. Neither the French nor ourselves could hold out for more than a few days longer against the pressures of political opinion and economic fact. Besides, as the decision to withdraw one battalion was being taken, the Prime Minister was struck down by illness. The strain of the last three weeks and of acting a part so completely out of character had by now caught up with him. The bouts of fever induced by his bile-duct trouble, which had occurred periodically since the beginning of October, had weakened him to the point of total exhaustion, and his doctors insisted that he could not carry on under the strain of office unless he now took a few weeks' rest. On November 21, No. 10 Downing Street therefore issued the astonishing announcement that the Prime Minister was to leave the country on doctors' orders and would be away for three weeks, during which time Mr. R. A. Butler would be in charge of the Government. On November 23 Eden and his wife left England for Jamaica.

The next day the U.N. General Assembly voted by 63 to 5 a resolution sponsored by the Afro-Asian nations which regretted the continued presence of British and French forces in Egypt and requested their withdrawal 'forthwith'. The debate which led to this vote was little less bitter and heated

than those which had preceded it. Pearson of Canada tried
without success to lower the temperature with some kindly
references to Britain and France. Then Paul Henri Spaak, the
Belgian Foreign Minister, moved an amendment to the resolution which omitted the demand for an immediate withdrawal.
Twenty-three nations voted for the Belgian amendment, including Australia, Canada, Denmark, Iceland, Italy, Luxem-
bourg, Netherlands, Norway, Portugal, Sweden, Turkey and
South Africa, plus, of course, Britain, France and Israel. But,
although this time the United States abstained, together with
the Latin American states, the combination of the Afro-Asian
group and the Soviet bloc mustered 37 votes against it. Thus
Spaak's valiant effort to take the pressure off us failed. Bitter
recriminations followed in Britain, and on November 27 over
100 Conservative M.P.s tabled a motion in the House of Commons 'deploring' the Assembly's demand for immediate withdrawal 'and the attitude of the United States of America, which
is gravely endangering the Atlantic Alliance'. Lloyd later told
the House on returning to London after the U.N. debate that
Lodge, in spite of his abstention, had stated that his interpretation of the Assembly's demand for withdrawal 'forthwith'
was 'a phased operation'! But this curious apologia for his
American colleague did nothing to assuage the fury of the Tory
back-benchers.

Still, whatever the Suez Group of Conservatives might think
of the United Nations and the Americans, the sands were un-
deniably running out for Britain and France, and there was no
more time to be bought by further argument, either with the
United States Government or with the U.N. On his visit to
Cairo, Hammarskjöld had found Nasser adamant in insisting
that the Anglo-French troops must be withdrawn before the
Egyptians would co-operate in clearing the Canal. With the
cease-fire in operation, Nasser was in a strong position to dictate
terms, knowing that, with world opinion so heavily against
Britain and France, they would not dare to resume their advance down the Canal. To tighten the screw still further, he

had ordered the expulsion from Egypt of all British and French citizens and had interned our civilian contractors who were operating the British base under the 1954 Agreement. And he had told Hammarskjöld that, while he was prepared to let U.N. salvage teams clear the Canal, this could only be started after British and French forces had left Port Said.

Lloyd had tried with all his might, while he was in New York, to buy a longer stay for our troops, if only to clear the Port Said end of the Canal, which they had already begun to do. But Hammarskjöld had no leeway to negotiate and Lloyd was forced to accept defeat. The task of clearance was to be entrusted to the Secretary-General, and this meant that we must clear out of Port Said without delay. On this same occasion, Lloyd had also raised with Hammarskjöld the question of resuming negotiations about the future of the Canal, suggesting that the Eighteen-Power proposals should form the basis of any resumed discussions. But to no avail. Hammarskjöld pointed out that Egypt had already rejected these proposals before the fighting started, and that the talks between Fawzi, Pineau and Lloyd had in any case reached agreement on a different approach. The best that Egypt might now be brought to accept would be a reversion to this agreement.

Thus, when Lloyd reported to the House of Commons on November 29, it was clear that his efforts in New York had been an almost total failure and that Britain had accepted, for herself at any rate, the need for early and complete withdrawal from Egypt. Trying to make the best of a miserable situation, he said that within a fortnight an 'organised military force' of over 4,000 men, drawn from different U.N. member states—India, Indonesia, Brazil, Colombia and the Scandinavian countries—would be established on Egyptian soil under the command of General Burns. He could not say anything for the time being about an Anglo-French withdrawal; but he was to have talks with the French Foreign Minister in London on the following day, and would make a further statement to the House after the week-end.

Lloyd and Pineau met over the week-end to consider the impasse which they had reached. Much as it went against the grain to admit it, both men knew that to continue to defy the United States and the U.N. spelled ruin for both their countries. There was no way out but retreat. It might be possible as a face-saver to make the withdrawal a phased operation to coincide with the build-up of the U.N. Emergency Force. But the phasing could not be spread over more than three weeks, and it was agreed that all British and French troops should be out of Egypt by December 22. Eisenhower was immediately notified of this decision, and on the same day, fulfilling his part of the bargain, he announced that he had authorised American oil companies to work together to supply oil to Europe.

The bitter pill had been swallowed at last, and on Monday, December 3, Lloyd rose to the Despatch Box to announce the fact to a tense House of Commons. In an abnormally long and argumentative statement, he tried to justify once more the decision to intervene, which, he claimed, had stopped the war between Egypt and Israel from spreading and had caused a serious reverse to Russian plans in the Middle East! But all his disingenuous phrases could not conceal the humiliation of the Government in having to admit that, along with their French allies, they had 'come to the conclusion that the withdrawal of their forces in the Port Said area can now be carried out without delay', and that they had 'instructed the Allied C.-in-C., General Keightley, to seek agreement with the United Nations Commander, General Burns, on a time-table for complete withdrawal'. Lloyd added that he was satisfied that the U.N. Secretary-General would tackle the task of clearing the Suez Canal speedily and effectively. As to the future, Hammarskjöld was to seek to get negotiations resumed on the basis of the Six Principles of the Security Council's resolution of October 13 and of his exchange of letters with Fawzi.

This announcement was greeted with jeers and ironical cheers from the Labour benches, while the Conservatives for

the most part sat in angry silence. For the Opposition, Aneurin
Bevan mocked the Foreign Secretary's claim that the Government had succeeded in what they set out to do. 'We sympathise,'
he said, 'with the Right Honourable and Learned Gentleman
in having to sound the bugle of advance to cover his retreat.'
Adding to Lloyd's discomfiture, Charles Waterhouse from the
Conservative back benches spoke of the failure of the Government, although he blamed this largely on the Labour Party's
pressures. Julian Amery went further and described the withdrawal as 'humiliating'. And no sooner had Lloyd denied this
than another Conservative M.P., Sir Ian Horobin, jumped up
to ask whether 'now that we have agreed to withdraw our army
from Egypt with no effective safeguards for our vital interests,
the necessary American consent will be forthcoming in due
course to bringing back our Prime Minister from Jamaica'.

Over the next three days the House of Commons held a
financial and political inquest on the Suez War. In the course
of these further exchanges, the Opposition managed to wring
from the Minister of Defence the extraordinary admission that
Britain had known that Israel was going to attack Egypt two or
three days before the event. Replying to a Labour back-bencher,
Colonel George Wigg, Head stated that 'On October 26 the
Government were informed by Her Majesty's Ambassador in
Tel Aviv that mobilisation of the Israeli forces had begun. During the next two days further information was received
indicating that Israeli forces were concentrating in the Negev.'
Up till this moment Government spokesmen had stuck rigidly
to the pretence that they had been led to believe that Israel
was threatening Jordan and not Egypt. Now, however, Head
was admitting something very different; and Wigg, sensing the
significance of the Minister's words, pressed him to say
whether or not he knew when the Israeli operation was to begin and what was to be its scope. Head now allowed himself
to be drawn still further, saying that 'the possibility of an
Israeli attack on Egypt had been in the mind of the Government for some considerable time, and that 'our first true know-

ledge that it was going to take place was when we were informed about the mobilisation'. In other words, the Government were now saying that they had had three days' notice that Israel was going to attack Egypt.

Although this was still by no means the whole truth, at least it was an improvement on the spurious pretences which had been offered up by every other Government spokesman hitherto. Yet, surprisingly enough, it was scarcely mentioned in the rest of the two days' debate. Opposition Members fell back on the old familiar charges of collusion with France and Israel and of deception of America and the Commonwealth. The equally familiar semi-rebuttals were made by Ministers. Apart from an account by Macmillan of the critical state of the nation's finances and of the perilous fall in our gold and dollar reserves, nothing new was said. And the vote at the end gave the Government its usual comfortable majority, with only a small assortment of the Suez Group declining to support the motion approving 'the policy of Her Majesty's Government as outlined by the Foreign Secretary on December 3'.

Still, however they might vote to keep the Government in power, the real feelings of probably a third of the Conservative back-benchers had been expressed by Messrs. Amery, Waterhouse and Horobin. They felt betrayed and humiliated and they were looking for a scapegoat. But, despite Horobin's vicious personal jibe, their quarry was not to be Eden. He was too ill, and besides, up to the point of his enforced departure, the Government had appeared to be standing firm against any general withdrawal. As for Lloyd, it was generally known that he had obeyed orders from start to finish. He was neither the instigator of the advance nor the architect of the retreat. And Harold Macmillan had cleverly stayed in the shadows throughout, save for his one histrionic display in the economic debate following the cease-fire. On the other hand, Rab Butler had given the order to retreat after Eden's departure. He was known never to have been in favour of our going into Egypt, and he had taken the first opportunity of getting us out. He had always been regarded as a 'leftist' in the Party, both on foreign and home affairs. In the myopic eyes of the Tory die-hards, Butler had helped to give India away and had revamped Conservative policy after 1945 so that it was indistinguishable from pale pink Socialism; and now he was accused of having given in to blackmail from America and the United Nations and surrendered the last position of strength from which we might have negotiated a settlement of the Suez Canal question on our terms.

Butler was therefore marked out as the Suez Group's chosen scapegoat and, when Eden's health forced him to resign as Prime Minister some five weeks later, these malignant men saw to it that his name should on no account be recommended to the Queen as the successor. Nor was this all. Not only did his conduct of affairs serve to consolidate the long-nurtured enmity of the Tory Right, but his loyal, if sometimes apparently unenthusiastic, efforts to defend the Government in debate had left a feeling of disenchantment among those Conservatives who had been opposed to our intervention from the start. Thus, by trying to do his duty to his colleagues and his Party, the unfortunate Butler contrived to get the worst of every world. And though he continued to hold high office for another eight years, he never really recovered from the wounds then inflicted on him—a bitter price for being loyal to a fault.

In a different way, I was to pay a bitter price myself for my action in resigning from the Government. This was because, both at the time and so long as any of the chief protagonists of the Suez War held office, I was precluded from giving the real reasons for my resignation. Had I been able to do so, I have no doubt that the unhappy breach with my constituency Association, which led to my leaving the House of Commons altogether, would not have occurred.

Even so, this breach might have been avoided had it not

been for the fact that a meeting of the Melton Conservative Executive had been scheduled for the day after my resignation was published. I had earlier warned the President and Chairman of the Melton Conservative Association, the Duke of Rutland and Donald Byford, of my impending resignation before it was announced. And on Sunday, November 4, when my letter to the Prime Minister was published in the Press, I met them both to explain that I was not in a position to give my reasons at any foreseeable time in the future, but that I would, in due course, nevertheless seek a vote of confidence at a General Meeting of all members of my Association. However, I had given the Prime Minister my solemn pledge that I would do nothing further to 'rock the boat' at this critical moment and, in particular, would not make any public statement either in Parliament or to my constituents. The duration of my silence would depend largely on the course of our military operations, which would probably mean that I would not be able to make any statement for another week or so. Meanwhile, I asked, bearing in mind that a meeting of the Melton Executive Committee had already been scheduled for the next evening, that judgment should be suspended by the Association on the merits or demerits of my resignation. If there were any danger that this self-denying ordinance would not be observed at the Executive's meeting, then I must insist on my right to be present.

Rutland agreed that all this was perfectly reasonable, as did Byford. They both felt that it would be a grave error to pronounce any judgment at this stage and that, if only because my presence would be certain to provoke discussion, it would be better for me to stay away from the meeting. On that note we parted. But at about eleven o'clock the following evening Rutland telephoned to ask in agitated tones whether he and Byford could come and see me right away. When they arrived half an hour later I could see from their faces that the meeting had gone badly amiss.

The Executive Committee, they said, had stampeded the

Chair. Several of them had been at the Party Conference, and they could not understand how I could make so belligerent a speech there and, when belligerent action followed, resign from the Government. Refusing to observe silence, they had insisted on sending a telegram to the Prime Minister which ranged them firmly on his side and against me. For good measure, copies of the telegram had then been given to the newspaper reporters from the national, as well as the local, Press who were gathered outside the conference room in the expectation that some startling news might emerge from this unhappily-timed gathering.

When they had finished their account of the meeting, I asked Rutland and Byford what they and the Executive Committee would do if I were to obtain a vote of confidence from a General Meeting of the Association. Byford said he could not answer such a hypothetical question! But Rutland, more straightforwardly, replied that in such an event he, and no doubt the rest of the Executive, would feel called upon to resign.

It was 'heads they won, tails I lost'. For if I won the vote of confidence, I would lose my Executive and be left with no organisation. My only hope was to tell the whole sordid story of what had happened since Llandudno. Nothing less than this would offer sufficient grounds for the Executive to climb down and carry on. Yet I could not tell the whole story at that stage without inflicting incalculable damage on the Government, and hence on the country. The more I thought about it, the more impossible my situation seemed to be. And on the following day I asked Rutland and Byford to tell the Association that I would resign from the constituency and so give them the opportunity to find a new M.P., untarnished by the Suez affair, to whom they could give their united backing.

One final personal problem remained. Should I, when the dust had cleared from the scene of conflict, make the traditional personal statement of a resigning Minister to the House of Commons? Or should I bow out of public life in total silence?

F

If I said nothing, it would look odd and might suggest that there was something to hide. This would deepen the widespread suspicion of collusion. Yet if I made a statement, what could I say? Three times I tried my hand at drafting something, toning each draft down as I went, progressively eliminating accusations and imputations and carefully avoiding anything which might hint at our collusion, so that the last draft became little more than a catalogue of pious regrets over the Government's actions. Still, since Parliamentary tradition required me to say something, I decided to go ahead with my final watered-down version and arranged with the Government Whips' Office to make the statement on November 13.

No sooner had I made this arrangement than I received a summons to call on Macmillan at his official residence in No. 11, Downing Street. At his request, I showed him the text of my intended statement. When he had finished reading it, he shook his head and, in solemn and almost funereal tones, he said, 'This is very damaging. It could easily bring down the Government, and for you, dear boy, it will do irreparable harm.' Then, after pausing for dramatic effect, he went on, 'Why say anything at all? You have already been proved right and we have been proved wrong. You have also done the right thing by resigning and, if you keep silent now, you will be revered and rewarded. You will lead the Party one day.'

At that moment I wanted to be quit of politics and all the hypocrisy that seemed to go with it. I did not even stop to argue, and, picking up my speech, walked silently from the room. Outside in the street, I tore my notes up and stuffed them down a drain. It seemed a fitting gesture.

Unlike Eden and his Ministers, the French Government had never felt any qualms about the collusive aspect of the Suez operations. Almost immediately after the Israeli attack had started, Pineau admitted collusion in a talk with the American Ambassador in Paris, Douglas Dillon, and made no secret of the fact that Britain had been involved as well. Equally unequivocal were the French Government's replies to the charge that the Americans had been duped. On December 9 Mollet at a press conference frankly admitted the accusation, saying that Britain and France both knew that America would be opposed to their plans and that, if Eisenhower had been informed, he would have tried to stop them.

Thus, when Eden returned from Jamaica on December 14, it was to a situation even more confused and malodorous than when he had left England three weeks earlier. Nevertheless, he tried to put a brave face on it as he arrived at London Airport. As soon as his feet touched British soil, he proclaimed to a posse of waiting journalists that the Anglo-French intervention had brought the U.N. Emergency Force into being and had stopped the war from spreading and frustrated Russia's plans in the area. In fact, he contended, we had made it possible for every country concerned to 'take a fresh look and make a new effort to solve the problems that have beset the Middle

East for far too long'. But behind all this vainglorious bluster lay the knowledge that he had lost his personal war against Nasser and that his policy was in ruins. Worse still, in a single act of lunacy he had undone almost all the work which, as Foreign Secretary from 1951 onwards, he had done to promote peace, stability and understanding of Britain within the Arab world, and had left a legacy of bitterness and distrust which it would take probably another generation to overcome.

Then on December 20, before Parliament adjourned for the Christmas Recess, the Opposition staged one final attempt to extract the truth about Anglo-French collusion with Israel. Gaitskell led off by saying that Pineau had stated a few days before in the French National Assembly that France and Britain had laid their plans well in advance of the Israeli attack on Egypt, which was why the two countries were so fully prepared for the attack when it came. Was this not an admission, he demanded, that the Suez War had been planned beforehand and that this had formed the basis of the meeting between the two Prime Ministers on October 16? But Eden refused to be drawn. Ignoring Pineau's statement and in complete disregard of what his own Minister of Defence had said only a fortnight earlier, he insisted once again that the Government had been led to believe that Israel was threatening Jordan, with whom we had a treaty of alliance. And throughout almost all the rest of the debate he managed by means of this kind of double-talk to keep out of trouble. But then in the final exchanges he went a little too far. Under relentless pressure by the Opposition, he said that, while the Government knew there was a risk of the Israelis breaking out in other directions, 'there was not foreknowledge that Israel would attack Egypt'.

Apart from the earlier denial by Selwyn Lloyd at the height of the crisis that there had been any 'prior agreement' between Britain and Israel, Eden's response marked the only occasion when Ministers actually lied to the House of Commons'. Almost every other statement is open to the charge of disingenuousness, and Ministers certainly sought to cover up their misdeeds in this connexion by every possible evasion. But, largely by using the old Parliamentary dodge of answering the question that was not asked, they managed—with these exceptions—to avoid saying anything that was strictly untrue. And although unhappily Eden's remark must remain on the record, coming as it did as such a blatant contradiction of Head's categorical statement fifteen days before, it may fairly be said to have been a slip of the tongue made under pressure by a man whose health was failing to the point where he could no longer exercise control over the House of Commons, still less the situation which he had created.

Proof of this grave deterioration of the Prime Minister's health came only a week later, when the fever which had laid Eden low before returned, while he was spending the Christmas holiday at Chequers. On his doctor's advice, he went to London to see two specialists, who agreed that, under pressure of work, the bouts of fever would become increasingly frequent. Since there could be no question of his being able to carry on working during such bouts, there was only one possible conclusion to be drawn. Accordingly, on January 9, Eden went to Buckingham Palace to tender his resignation as the Queen's First Minister. Nine days later he left for New Zealand at the invitation of her Prime Minister, Sidney Holland, to spend the rest of the winter months in the sunshine.

Shortly afterwards the final irony for me came in the form of a letter from the Chancellor of the Exchequer. To enable me to resign from the House of Commons, I had applied for the Chiltern Hundreds and had been duly appointed under the resounding title of 'Steward and Bailiff of the Manor of Northstead'. But I did not hold this curious sinecure for very long. Eden too was to retire from the House of Commons. And less than two months after my 'appointment', I was informed by the new Chancellor of the Exchequer that I was no longer a Steward of the Chiltern Hundreds, for my place had been taken by none other than 'the Right Honourable Sir Anthony Eden, K.G., M.C.'.

While this personal tragedy was being acted out to its final
bitter conclusion, steps were being taken to clear up the mess
which our abortive intervention had created in the Canal Zone.
The Anglo-French withdrawal continued and, despite one or
two hitches, was completed on schedule. The U.N. Emergency
Force under General Burns was progressively built up to its
full complement of around 4,000 men. And the Israelis began
to withdraw from the positions which they had captured in the
Sinai Peninsula, although it was not until three months later,
after Israel had obtained a guarantee that the U.N.E.F. would
remain indefinitely in the Gaza Strip and on the Tiran Strait,
that the Israeli evacuation was completed.

Determined efforts made through the Secretary-General of
the U.N. succeeded in saving at least half of the total number
of British citizens in Egypt from being expelled. It was pointed
out to the Egyptians that these people were for the most part
Maltese and Cypriots who had made their lives in Egypt and
had no connexions with the United Kingdom other than their
British passports. Terrible hardships would be inflicted on
them if they were forced to leave Egypt and to try to make a
new life elsewhere. To begin with, these powerful humanitarian arguments had no effect and by mid-December some
2,500 British and 3,500 French citizens had had to leave the
country and abandon their possessions to the Government
sequestrator. But once it became clear that the Anglo-French
forces were in fact withdrawing from Port Said, the Egyptian
authorities relented; and in due course an agreement was made
to provide compensation for those who had lost their property.
At the same time the 450 British civilians who had been operating the British half of the base at Ismailia were released from
internment in exchange for 250 Egyptian soldiers whom we
had taken prisoner during the fighting in and around Port Said.
This exchange was completed on the eve of the final embarka-
tion of British troops.

Finally, the U.N. salvage teams moved in to begin the mam-
moth task of clearing the Canal. Some bitter feelings had been

aroused in Britain, and in France too, that our offer to help remove the blockships had not been accepted. Lord Hailsham, the First Lord of the Admiralty, feeling that the professional skill of the British Navy had been slighted, was moved to angry protest in a public speech. But any argument as to who could best clear the Canal was quite sterile at this stage. Clearance required Egyptian co-operation, and the Egyptians would not co-operate until those who had invaded their country had left. This was their ace of trumps, and it was not to be wondered at that they should play it. In any case, there is no reason to suppose that any unnecessary delays occurred in completing the clearance, which it was in every nation's interest to get done in the shortest possible time. Selwyn Lloyd himself went out of his way publicly to praise Hammarskjöld for his energy in this respect and for his wisdom in selecting Mr. John McCloy and General Wheeler, two distinguished American administrators, to direct the work of clearance.

While all this debris of disaster was being removed, a parallel effort was being made to work out a settlement of the Canal dispute with Egypt. In a desperate attempt to salvage something from the wreck of the Eden policy, Lloyd sought to take up the threads of negotiation from where they had been broken in October. He realised now all too clearly that he ought never to have allowed the agreement with Fawzi in New York to be thrown overboard in favour of the ill-fated attempt to settle the issue by force. And on December 19 he declared the Government's attitude towards future negotiations in these terms: 'The policy of the Government with regard to this matter is exactly as it stood at the end of the Security Council's debate, when the resolution was put forward endorsing the Six Principles and saying that we considered that the Eighteen-Power proposals were the best method of carrying out the Six Principles, but that we recognised that alternative methods could be put forward. In the letter sent by the Secretary-General to the Egyptian Government—I believe it was on October 24—*there is set out the broad lines of a scheme which,*

*if properly implemented and worked out in detail, could be
regarded as complying with these Six Principles'*, i.e. the
scheme providing for user participation which Fawzi had conceded.

But it was too late to revert to the agreement offered by
Fawzi in October. Too much had happened since the talks in
New York. The British attitude might be 'exactly as it stood'
then, but the Egyptian attitude had inevitably hardened. True,
Fawzi had replied to the Secretary-General's letter on November 2 to confirm his acceptance of the scheme agreed with
Pineau and Lloyd. But this was before British and French
forces had dropped out of the sky to invade and occupy
Egyptian territory. Now it was impossible for the Egyptian
Government to go back to that agreement as if nothing had
happened since it was put forward. Public opinion would not
accept such concessions to those who had invaded Egyptian
soil at the side of the arch-enemy, Israel. Nor would the Army,
smarting as it was under the lash of a humiliating defeat at
Israel's hands. Besides, the ineptitude of Britain's and France's
intervention had enormously strengthened Egypt's position
internationally. She now had friends everywhere; the U.N.
were on her side; and the anger of the Arab world over Nasser's
sudden decision to nationalise the Suez Canal Company without consultation with the Arab League had now melted in the
warm glow of brotherhood and sympathy which had flowed
from all Arab hearts when Egypt was attacked by the 'Western
imperialists and their Israeli stooges'. No true Arab nationalist
would now dare to resume the pressure to make concessions
over the Canal issue which Iraq and Saudi Arabia had exerted
before hostilities began. And all true Arab nationalists would
expect Egypt to stand on her absolute rights to run the Canal
in her own way and to force the West to accept her terms.

Not surprisingly, therefore, after three months of abortive
efforts by Britain and France, now backed by the United States,
to re-establish the principle of international control, the
Egyptians unilaterally announced their terms for a settlement.

The Canal was to be operated and managed by the Egyptian Suez Canal Authority; compensation would be paid to the former Company; tolls must be paid to the Egyptian Authority; and freedom of transit would be guaranteed in accordance with the 1888 Convention. Israeli ships would therefore still be denied passage on security grounds. And the users, whose rights to be represented in the Canal's administration had been recognised in the October agreement, were now to be left out of account. In sum, defying the insistent demands of Britain and France, the Egyptians were making sure that unfettered control of the Canal should be in their hands.

This was a bitter pill for us to swallow, and when three weeks after the Egyptian announcement the Canal was reopened to shipping on April 9, Britain, France and America made one last effort to squeeze some concession out of Egypt on behalf of the users' interests. They advised their shipowners not to use the Canal for the time being and to continue to route their ships round the Cape of Good Hope. But when they sought to persuade other user nations to follow suit at a meeting of the Users' Association on April 30, it soon became clear that a large majority were against attempting such a boycott. Even if it could be effective at this stage, it would be too expensive. So on May 13 the Prime Minister announced that the Government would no longer advise British shipping against using the Canal. In a subsequent debate in the House of Commons, Macmillan sought to gloss over this final surrender by saying that, in respect of the day-to-day working of the Canal, the Egyptian terms were not so very far from the Six Principles on which we had taken our stand! He also said that Britain would continue to work for an arrangement which would insulate the Canal from the politics of any one country, and he tried to make out that Nasser's negotiating position was a lot weaker than some people might think. Where was Egypt to get the vast sums needed for development projects, such as the Aswan High Dam? The Russians had been generous in supplying arms, but not money. Therefore 'the only source from which Colonel Nasser can hope to find this money is the West' was his extraordinary conclusion.

Lloyd struck a different note. No doubt realising that our negotiating position had been virtually destroyed and that Nasser held all the cards, he sought comfort in the belief that, by such devices as building and operating super-tankers around the Cape route, Western Europe's dependence on the Canal could be greatly diminished. 'It must be brought home to those who have physical control of the Canal,' he said, 'that their asset may easily be a wasting one.' Then, whistling on to keep up the courage of his dismayed supporters, he proceeded to take credit for having brought a new era of peace to the Middle East! 'The myth of Egyptian military power has been exploded,' he said, 'the United Nations force is in position and Israel feels more secure for the time being against Egyptian attack.' And all this was due to the Anglo-French intervention!

As it became more and more obvious with the passage of time that the last word about the Canal issue had been said by Egypt, Government spokesmen pointed with increasing emphasis to other more 'encouraging' developments in the Middle East. The United States had adopted a more decisive policy, it was claimed. The Eisenhower doctrine of helping the Arab states to resist Communism had been introduced in January. Then there was America's welcome, though belated, decision to join the Military Committee of the Baghdad Pact. The Arab world, too, had woken up to the dangers of Russian penetration. Saudi Arabia, Iraq and Jordan were forgetting old feuds and working together to resist Communist conspiracies and pressures; and King Hussein, by defeating an attempted *coup d'état* in April, 1957, had delivered a serious setback to Nasser's 'plots' to take over Jordan. In fact, the Prime Minister actually contended on one occasion that, thanks to the lead which we and the French had given in the previous autumn, 'the whole pattern of the Middle East countries is changing and the forces of order and anti-Communism are recovering their strength'.

I must confess to having been to some extent similarly deceived myself by the apparent recovery of the pro-Western forces in the Arab world in the spring of 1957, although from what I saw and heard on the spot it was clear that any strengthening of their position was in spite of, and not because of, the Suez War. But how wrong these optimistic estimates were was shown a year later, when revolutions in Lebanon and Iraq swept away the régimes of Camille Chamoun and Nuri es-Said, and a threat to repeat the dose in Jordan was only prevented by the arrival of a British paratroop brigade, sent at Hussein's urgent request. We had sown the wind of bitterness and we were to reap the whirlwind of revenge and rebellion. The friends whom we had claimed to uphold were destroyed and the man whom we had set out to crush as their 'enemy' and ours had triumphed. By making Nasser a martyr and a hero, we had raised him to a pinnacle of power and prestige unknown in the Arab world since the beginning of the eighteenth century, when Mohammed Ali defied the combined pressures of the Ottoman Sultan and of Lord Palmerston's England to enthrone himself as the independent ruler of renascent Egypt.

Appendices

Convention Between Great Britain, Germany, Austria-Hungary, Spain, France, Italy, The Netherlands, Russia, and Turkey, respecting the Free Navigation of the Suez Maritime Canal[1]

Signed at Constantinople, 29 October 1888

Article I

The Suez Maritime Canal shall always be free and open, in time of war as in time of peace, to every vessel of commerce or of war, without distinction of flag.

Consequently, the High Contracting Parties agree not in any way to interfere with the free use of the Canal, in time of war as in time of peace.

The Canal shall never be subjected to the exercise of the right of blockade.

Article II

The High Contracting Parties, recognising that the Fresh-Water Canal is indispensable to the Maritime Canal, take note of the engagements of His Highness the Khedive towards the

[1] Commercial No. 2 (1889) (Suez Canal), C. 5623.

Universal Suez Canal Company as regards the Fresh-Water Canal; which engagements are stipulated in a Convention bearing the date of 18th March, 1863, containing an *exposé* and four Articles.

They undertake not to interfere in any way with the security of that Canal and its branches, the working of which shall not be exposed to any attempt at obstruction.

ARTICLE III

The High Contracting Parties likewise undertake to respect the plant, establishments, buildings, and works of the Maritime Canal and of the Fresh-Water Canal.

ARTICLE IV

The Maritime Canal remaining open in time of war as a free passage, even to the ships of war of belligerents, according to the terms of Article I of the present Treaty, the High Contracting Parties agree that no right of war, no act of hostility, nor any act having for its object to obstruct the free navigation of the Canal shall be committed in the Canal and its ports of access, as well as within a radius of three marine miles from those parts, even though the Ottoman Empire should be one of the belligerent Powers.

Vessels of war of belligerents shall not revictual or take in stores in the Canal and its ports of access, except in so far as may be strictly necessary. The transit of the aforesaid vessels through the Canal shall be effected with the least possible delay, in accordance with the Regulations in force, and without any other intermission than that resulting from the necessities of the service.

Their stay at Port Said and in the roadstead of Suez shall not exceed twenty-four hours, except in cases of distress. In such case they shall be bound to leave as soon as possible. An interval of twenty-four hours shall always elapse between the sailing of a belligerent ship from one of the ports of access and the departure of a ship belonging to the hostile Power.

ARTICLE V

In time of war belligerent Powers shall not disembark nor embark within the Canal and its ports of access either troops, munitions, or materials of war. But in case of an accidental hindrance in the Canal, men may be embarked or disembarked at the ports of access by detachments not exceeding 1,000 men, with a corresponding amount of war material.

ARTICLE VI

Prizes shall be subjected, in all respects, to the same rules as the vessels of war of belligerents.

ARTICLE VII

The Powers shall not keep any vessel of war in the waters of the Canal (including Lake Timsah and the Bitter Lakes).

Nevertheless, they may station vessels of war in the ports of access of Port Said and Suez, the number of which shall not exceed two for each Power.

This right shall not be exercised by belligerents.

ARTICLE VIII

The Agents in Egypt of the Signatory Powers of the present Treaty shall be charged to watch over its execution. In case of any event threatening the security of the free passage of the Canal, they shall meet on the summons of three of their number under the presidency of their Doyen, in order to proceed to the necessary verifications. They shall inform the Khedivial Government of the danger which they may have perceived, in order that that Government may take proper steps to insure the protection and the free use of the Canal. Under any circumstances, they shall meet once a year to take note of the due execution of the Treaty.

The last-mentioned meetings shall take place under the presidency of a Special Commissioner nominated for that purpose by the Imperial Ottoman Government. A Commissioner of the Khedive may also take part in the meeting, and may preside over it in case of the absence of the Ottoman Commissioner.

They shall especially demand the suppression of any work or the dispersion of any assemblage on either bank of the Canal, the object or effect of which might be to interfere with the liberty and the entire security of the navigation.

ARTICLE IX

The Egyptian Government shall, within the limits of its powers resulting from the Firmans, and under the conditions provided for in the present Treaty, take the necessary measures for insuring the execution of the said Treaty.

In case the Egyptian Government shall not have sufficient means at its disposal, it shall call upon the Imperial Ottoman Government, which shall take the necessary measures to respond to such appeal; shall give notice thereof to the Signatory Powers of the Declaration of London of the 17th March, 1885; and shall, if necessary, concert with them on the subject.

The provisions of Articles IV, V, VII, and VIII shall not interfere with the measures which shall be taken in virtue of the present Article.

ARTICLE X

Similarly, the provisions of Articles IV, V, VII, and VIII shall not interfere with the measures which His Majesty the Sultan and His Highness the Khedive, in the name of His Imperial Majesty, and within the limits of the Firmans granted, might find it necessary to take for securing by their own forces the defence of Egypt and the maintenance of public order.

In case His Imperial Majesty the Sultan, or His Highness the Khedive, should find it necessary to avail themselves of the exception for which this Article provides, the Signatory Powers of the Declaration of London shall be notified thereof by the Imperial Ottoman Government.

It is likewise understood that the provisions of the four Articles aforesaid shall in no case occasion any obstacle to the measures which the Imperial Ottoman Government may think it necessary to take in order to insure by its own forces the defence of its other possessions situated on the eastern coast of the Red Sea.

ARTICLE XI

The measures which shall be taken in the cases provided for by Articles IX and X of the present Treaty shall not interfere with the free use of the Canal. In the same cases, the erection of permanent fortifications contrary to the provisions of Article VIII is prohibited.

ARTICLE XII

The High Contracting Parties, by application of the principle of equality as regards the free use of the Canal, a principle which forms one of the bases of the present Treaty, agree that none of them shall endeavour to obtain with respect to the Canal territorial or commercial advantages or privileges in any international arrangements which may be concluded. Moreover, the rights of Turkey as the territorial Power are reserved.

ARTICLE XIII

With the exception of the obligations expressly provided by the clauses of the present Treaty, the sovereign rights of His Imperial Majesty the Sultan and the rights and immunities of His Highness the Khedive, resulting from the Firmans, are in no way affected.

ARTICLE XIV

The High Contracting Parties agree that the engagements resulting from the present Treaty shall not be limited by the duration of the Acts of Concession of the Universal Suez Canal Company.

ARTICLE XV

The stipulations of the present Treaty shall not interfere with the sanitary measures in force in Egypt.

ARTICLE XVI

The High Contracting Parties undertake to bring the present Treaty to the knowledge of the States which have not signed it, inviting them to accede to it.

ARTICLE XVII

The present Treaty shall be ratified, and the ratifications shall be exchanged at Constantinople within the space of one month, or sooner if possible.

In faith of which the respective Plenipotentiaries have signed the present Treaty, and have affixed to it the seal of their arms.

> Done at Constantinople the 29th day of the month of October of the year 1888.

APPENDIX II

THE TRIPARTITE DECLARATION:
FRANCE, UNITED KINGDOM, UNITED STATES
MAY 25, 1950

'1. The three Governments recognise that the Arab States and Israel all need to maintain a certain level of armed forces for the purposes of assuring their internal security and their legitimate self-defence and to permit them to play their part in the defence of the area as a whole. All applications for arms or war material for these countries will be considered in the light of these principles. In this connection the three Governments wish to recall and reaffirm the terms of the statements made by their representatives on the Security Council on 4th August, 1949, in which they declared their opposition to the development of an arms race between the Arab States and Israel.

'2. The three Governments declare that assurances have been received from all the States in question to which they permit arms to be supplied from their countries that the purchasing State does not intend to undertake any act of aggression against any other State. Similar assurances will be requested from any other States in the area to which they permit arms to be supplied in the future.

'3. The three Governments take this opportunity of declaring their deep interest in and their desire to promote the establishment and maintenance of peace and stability in the area, and their unalterable opposition to the use of force or threat of force between any of the States in that area. The three Governments, should they find that any of these States was preparing to violate frontiers or armistice lines, would, consistently with their obligations as members of the United Nations, immediately take action, both within and outside the United Nations, to prevent such violation.'

Assurances in the terms of paragraph 2 of the statement were received by the United Kingdom from Egypt, Jordan, Iraq and Saudi Arabia; by the United States from Egypt, Saudi Arabia, Israel and Syria; and by France from Syria and the Lebanon.

APPENDIX III

EGYPTIAN LAW NATIONALISING THE SUEZ CANAL COMPANY, 26 JULY 1956[1]

In the name of the Nation,
The President of the Republic,

Considering the firmans of 30 November 1854 and 5 January 1956 [1856] concerning the administration of traffic

[1] Translated from *La Bourse Egyptienne*, July 27, 1956.

services through the Suez Canal and the establishment of an Egyptian joint stock company for its exploitation;

Considering law no. 129 of 1947 concerning public utility concessions;

Considering law no. 317 of 1952 concerning individual contracts of work;

Considering law no. 26 of 1954 concerning joint stock companies, shareholders' companies and limited liability companies;

Considering the opinion of the Council of State;

Promulgates the following law : —

ARTICLE I

The International Company of the Suez Maritime Canal (Egyptian Joint Stock Company) is hereby nationalised. Its assets and liabilities revert to the State and the councils and committees at present responsible for its administration are dissolved.

The shareholders and holders of founders' shares will be compensated for the stock and shares which they own on the basis of their closing price on the Paris Bourse immediately preceding the date on which this law enters into force.

Payment of this compensation will be made when all the assets of the nationalised company have been fully handed over to the State.

ARTICLE II

The administration of traffic services through the Suez Canal will be carried out by an independent body with the legal status of a Corporation; it will be attached to the Ministry of Commerce. An order of the President of the Republic will fix the composition of this body and the payment to be made to its members. This body will have full powers necessary for controlling this service and will not be subject to administrative routine and regulations.

Subject to the right of the Cour des Comptes to supervise its final accounts, this body will have an independent budget which will be drawn up according to the rules established by commercial legislation. The financial year will begin on 1 July and end on 30 June of each year. The budget and final accounts will be approved by an order of the President of the Republic. The first financial year will begin on the date on which this law enters into force and will end on 30 June 1957.

The body may delegate to one or more of its members the responsibility for carrying out its decisions or any duties it may assign to them.

It may set up technical committees consisting of its members or other qualified persons whose services it will use for purposes of research and study.

The chairman of the body will act as its representative before judicial, governmental and other authorities. He will represent it in its relations with third parties.

ARTICLE III

The funds of the nationalised company and its rights in Egypt and abroad are hereby frozen. Banks, institutions and private persons are forbidden to dispose of these assets in any way, to pay out any sum whatever or to meet claims for payment without previous sanction by the body envisaged in Article II.

ARTICLE IV

The body will retain the services of the officials of the nationalised company and of its employees and manual workers. These must continue their work and are forbidden to leave their employment or to abandon it in any way or for any reason whatsoever without the previous permission of the body envisaged in Article II.

ARTICLE V

Any breach of the terms of Article III will be punished

with imprisonment and a fine equal to three times the value of the sum involved. Any breach of the terms of Article IV will be punished with imprisonment; the offender will, in addition, be deprived of any right to a gratuity, pension or compensation.

ARTICLE VI

This decision will be published in the *Journal Officiel*. It will have the force of law and will be effective from the date of its publication.

The Minister of Commerce will make the orders necessary for its implementation. This decision will bear the seal of the State and will be implemented as a law of the State.

APPENDIX IV

THE 18-POWER PROPOSALS OF THE FIRST LONDON CONFERENCE, 16-23 AUGUST 1956

The following is the final text of the proposal which was endorsed by the Delegates of Australia, Denmark, Ethiopia, France, the Federal Republic of Germany, Iran, Italy, Japan, Netherlands, New Zealand, Norway, Pakistan, Portugal, Sweden, Turkey, the United Kingdom, the United States and, subject to the statement reproduced under Item 7 (ii), Spain : —

The Governments approving this Statement, being participants in the London Conference on the Suez Canal : —

Concerned by the grave situation regarding the Suez Canal;

Seeking a peaceful solution in conformity with the purposes and principles of the United Nations; and

Recognising that an adequate solution must, on the one hand, respect the sovereign rights of Egypt, including its rights to just and fair compensation for the use of the Canal, and, on the other hand, safeguard the Suez Canal as an international waterway in accordance with the Suez Canal Convention of 29th October, 1888;

Assuming for the purposes of this statement that just and fair compensation will be paid to the Universal Company of the Suez Maritime Canal, and that the necessary arrangements for such compensation, including a provision for arbitration in the event of disagreement, will be covered by the final settlement contemplated below

Join in this expression of their views:—

1. They affirm that, as stated in the Preamble of the Convention of 1888, there should be established 'a definite system destined to guarantee at all times, and for all the Powers, the free use of the Suez Maritime Canal'.

2. Such a system which would be established with due regard to the sovereign rights of Egypt, should assure:—

   (*a*) Efficient and dependable operation, maintenance and development of the Canal as a free, open and secure international waterway in accordance with the principles of the Convention of 1888.

   (*b*) Insulation of the operation of the Canal from the influence of the politics of any nation.

   (*c*) A return to Egypt for the use of the Suez Canal which will be fair and equitable and increasing with enlargements of its capacity and greater use.

   (*d*) Canal tolls as low as is consistent with the foregoing requirements and, except for (*c*) above, no profit.

3. To achieve these results on a permanent and reliable basis there should be established by a Convention to be negotiated with Egypt:—

   (*a*) Institutional arrangements for co-operation between Egypt and other interested nations in the operation, maintenance and development of the Canal and for harmonising and safeguarding their respective interests in the Canal. To this end, operating, maintaining and developing the Canal and enlarging it so as to increase the volume of traffic in the interest of the world trade and of Egypt, would be the responsibility of a Suez Canal Board. Egypt would grant this Board all rights and facilities appropriate to its functioning as here outlined. The status of the Board would be defined in the above-mentioned Convention.

The members of the Board, in addition to Egypt, would be other States chosen in a manner to be agreed upon from among the States parties to the Convention with due regard to use, pattern of trade and geographical distribution; the composition of the Board to be such as to assure that its responsibilities would be discharged solely with a view to achieving the best possible operating results without political motivation in favour of, or in prejudice against, any user of the Canal.

The Board would make periodic reports to the United Nations.

(b) An Arbitral Commission to settle any disputes as to the equitable return to Egypt or other matters arising in the operation of the Canal.

(c) Effective sanctions for any violation of the Convention by any party to it, or any other nation, including provisions for treating any use or threat of force to interfere with the use or operation of the Canal as a threat to the peace and a violation of the purposes and principles of the United Nations Charter.

(d) Provisions for appropriate association with the United Nations and for review as may be necessary.

APPENDIX V

DRAFT RESOLUTION SUBMITTED BY GREAT BRITAIN AND FRANCE TO THE SECURITY COUNCIL, 13 OCTOBER 1956

The Security Council,
  Noting the declarations made before it and the accounts of the development of the exploratory conversations on the Suez

question given by the Secretary-General of the United Nations and the Foreign Ministers of Egypt, France and the United Kingdom;

Agrees that any settlement of the Suez question should meet the following requirements:

(1) there should be free and open transit through the Canal without discrimination, overt or covert—this covers both political and technical aspects;

(2) the sovereignty of Egypt should be respected;

(3) the operation of the Canal should be insulated from the politics of any country;

(4) the manner of fixing tolls and charges should be decided by agreement between Egypt and the users;

(5) a fair proportion of the dues should be allotted to development;

(6) in case of disputes, unresolved affairs between the Suez Canal Company and the Egyptian Government should be settled by arbitration with suitable terms of reference and suitable provisions for the payment of sums found to be due;

Considers that the proposals of the Eighteen Powers correspond to the reuirements set out above and are suitably designed to bring about a settlement of the Suez Canal question by peaceful means in conformity with justice;

Notes that the Egyptian Government, while declaring its readiness in the exploratory conversations to accept the principle of organised collaboration between an Egyptian Authority and the users, has not yet formulated sufficiently precise proposals to meet the requirements set out above;

Invites the Governments of Egypt, France and the United Kingdom to continue their interchanges and in this connexion *invites* the Egyptian Government to make known promptly its proposals for a system meeting the requirements set out above and providing guarantees to the users not less effective than those sought by the proposals of the Eighteen Powers;

Considers that, pending the conclusion of an agreement for the definite settlement of the régime of the Suez Canal on the basis of the requirements set out above, the Suez Canal Users' Association, which has been qualified to receive the dues payable by ships belonging to its members, and the competent Egyptian authorities should co-operate to ensure the satisfactory operation of the Canal and free and open transit through the Canal in accordance with the 1888 Convention.

APPENDIX VI

EXCHANGE OF NOTES BETWEEN THE SECRETARY-GENERAL OF THE UNITED NATIONS AND THE EGYPTIAN MINISTER OF FOREIGN AFFAIRS CONCERNING THE SUEZ CANAL, 24 OCTOBER AND 2 NOVEMBER 1956

24 October, 1956

Dear Dr. Fawzi,

You will remember that at the end of the private talks on Suez, trying to sum up what I understood as being the sense of the discussion, I covered not only the 'requirements', later approved by the Security Council, but also in a summary form arrangements that had been discussed as possible means of meeting those requirements. However, time then proved insufficient for a satisfactory exploration of those arrangements.

Before you left New York I raised with you the question of time and place for a resumption of the exploratory talks, in case the three Governments directly concerned would find that such further talks should be tried. As a follow up to these observations to which, so far, I have had no reactions either from you or from Mr. Selwyn Lloyd or M. Pineau, I would, for my own sake, wish to put on paper how I envisage the situation that would have to be studied at resumed exploratory talks, if they were to come about.

Again, what I do is not to put out any proposals on my own, nor try to formulate proposals made by you or any of the others. Just as I did at the end of the private talks in New York, I just wish, in my own words, to try to spell out what are my conclusions from the—entirely noncommittal—observations made in the course of the private talks, interpolating on some points in the light of my interpretation of the sense of the talks where they did not fully cover the ground. Whether you approve of my phrasing or not, I feel that it would be valuable to know if, in your view, I have correctly interpreted the conclusions from the tentative thinking which would provide the background for further explorations.

1. From the discussions I understood that the legal reaffirmation of all the obligations under the Constantinople Convention should not present any difficulty; this is a question of form, not of substance. I further understood that it would not present any difficulties to widen the obligations under the Convention to cover the questions of maximum of tolls (as at present); maintenance and development; reporting to the United Nations.

2. Nor should, if I understood the sense of the discussions correctly, the questions of the Canal Code and the regulations present any difficulties of substance, as I understood the situation to be that no revision of the Code or the regulations was envisaged which would lead to rules less adequate than the present Rules. I further understood that revisions would be subject to consultation.

3. Nor, in my understanding, should the question of tolls and charges present any difficulties, as, according to what emerged in the discussions, the manner of fixing tolls and charges would be subject to agreement, and as also the reservation of a certain part of the dues for development purposes would be subject to agreement.

4. Nor, in my understanding, should the principle of or-

ganised co-operation between an Egyptian Authority and the users give rise to any differences of views, while, on the other hand, it obviously represents a field where the arrangements to be made call for careful exploration in order to make sure that they would meet the three first requirements approved by the Security Council. The following points in the summing up of my understanding of the sense of the discussions refer to this question of implementation of an organised co-operation:

A. The co-operation requires obviously an organ on the Egyptian side (the authority in charge of the operation of the Canal), and a representation of the users, recognised by the Canal Authority (and the Egyptian Government) and entitled to speak for the users.

B. Provisions should be made for joint meetings between the Authority and the representation to all the extent necessary to effect the agreed co-operation.

C. Within the framework of the co-operation, the representation should be entitled to raise all matters affecting the users' rights or interests, for discussion and consultation or by way of complaint. The representation should, on the other hand, of course not, in exercising its functions, do this in such a way as to interfere with the administrative functions of the operating organ.

D. The co-operation which would develop on the basis of points A-C would not give satisfaction to the three first requirements approved by the Security Council unless completed with arrangements for fact-finding, reconciliation, recourse to appropriate juridical settlement of possible disputes and guarantees for execution of the results of reconciliation or juridical settlements of disputes.

E. (*a*) Fact-finding can be provided for by direct access for the Party concerned to a checking of relevant facts, or by a Standing (Joint) Organ, with appropriate representation for both parties;

(*b*) A Standing (Joint) Organ might also be considered for reconciliation;

(*c*) In case of unresolved differences, as to facts or other relevant questions, not resolved by the arrangements so far mentioned, recourse should be possible—as the case may be—to a Standing Local Organ for arbitration, set up in accordance with common practices, or to whatever other arbitration organ found necessary in the light of a further study of the character of the conflicts that may arise, or to the International Court of Justice (whose jurisdiction in this case of course should be mandatory), or to the Security Council (or whatever other organ of the United Nations that may be established under the rules of the Charter);

(*d*) Concerning the implementation of findings by a United Nations organ, normal rules should apply. In respect of the implementation of awards made by a Standing Organ for Arbitration, or by whatever other organ may be established for similar purposes, the parties should undertake the recognise the awards as binding, when rendered, and undertake to carry them out in good faith. In case of a complaint because of alleged non-compliance with an award, the same arbitration organ which gave the award, should register the fact of non-compliance. Such a 'constatation' would give the complaining party access to all normal forms of redress, but also the right to certain steps in self-protection, the possible scope of which should be subject to an agreement in principle; both sides, thus, in a case of a 'constatation', should be entitled to certain limited 'police action', even with recourse to further juridical procedures.

5. It was, finally, my understanding that the question covered by the requirement in Point 6 of the Security Council Resolution, would not give rise to special difficulties, as the

subject seems fairly well covered by the formulation of the principles itself.

Whether or not a set of arrangements will meet the first three requirements approved by the Security Council will, according to my understanding of the situation, depend on the reply to the questions under Point 4 above. That is true not only with an arrangement starting from the assumption of operation of the Canal by an Egyptian Authority, but also on the assumption that the operation of the Canal (in the narrow sense of the word) is organised in another way. If I have rightly interpreted the sense of the discussions as concerns specifically the questions of verification, recourse and enforcement (Point 4 (E)), and if, thus, no objection in principle is made a priori against arrangements as set down above, I would, from a legal and technical point of view—without raising here the political considerations which come into play—consider the framework sufficiently wide to make a further exploration of a possible basis for negotiations along the lines indicated worth trying.

I am sure you appreciate that whatever clarification you may give of your reaction to this interpretation of mine of the possibilities would be helpful for me in contacts with other parties—of the reactions of which I likewise need a more complete picture—and might smooth the way to progress beyond the point reached in the private talks.

> (Signed) Yours sincerely,
> DAG HAMMARSKJÖLD.

Egyptian Mission to the United Nations
New York, November 2, 1956.

Excellency,

I have the honour to transmit to you the following communication which I have just received from Dr. Mahmoud Fawzi:

'Dear Mr. Hammarskjöld,

'I have the honour to refer to your letter of 25 October, 1956. You will recall that on 29 October, I informed you through the Permanent Representative of Egypt, Ambassador Omar Loutfi, that it was under careful consideration and that I shall convey to you the result as soon as possible.

'I am now doing this; and am pleased to be able to tell you that, with the exception of the latter part of 'd' of sub-paragraph 'E' of Paragraph 4, we share with you the view that the framework you have outlined in your letter is sufficiently wide to make a further exploration for a possible basis for negotiation along the lines indicated in it is worth trying.

'Mahmoud Fawzi'.

Please accept, Your Excellency, the assurances of my highest consideration,

(Signed) OMAR LOUTFI,
Permanent Representative
of Egypt to the United
Nations

H.E. Mr. Dag Hammarskjöld,
Secretary-General of the United Nations.

APPENDIX VII

EDEN'S STATEMENT TO HOUSE OF COMMONS, OCTOBER 30, 1956

With your permission and that of the House I will make a statement. As the House will know for some time past the tension on the frontiers of Israel has been increasing. The growing military strength of Egypt has given rise to renewed apprehension, which the statements and actions of the Egyptian Government have further aggravated. The establishment of a joint military command between Egypt, Jordan and Syria, the renewed raids by guerrillas, culminating in the incursion of

Egyptian commandos on Sunday night had all produced a very dangerous situation.

Five days ago news was received that the Israel Government were taking certain measures of mobilisation. Her Majesty's Government at once instructed Her Majesty's Ambassador at Tel Aviv to make enquiries of the Israel Minister for Foreign Affairs and to urge restraint.

Meanwhile, President Eisenhower called for an immediate tripartite discussion between representatives of the United Kingdom, France and the United States. A meeting was held on October 28 in Washington and a second meeting took place on October 29.

While these discussions were proceeding, news was received last night that Israel forces had crossed the frontier and had penetrated deep into Egyptian territory. Later, further reports were received indicating that paratroops had been dropped. It appeared that the Israel spearhead was not far from the banks of the Suez Canal. From recent reports it also appears that air forces are in action in the neighbourhood of the Canal.

During the last few weeks Her Majesty's Government have thought it their duty, having regard to their obligations under the Anglo-Jordan Treaty, to give assurances both public and private of the intention to honour these obligations. Her Majesty's Ambassador in Tel Aviv late last night received an assurance that Israel would not attack Jordan.

My Right Honourable and Learned Friend the Foreign Secretary discussed the situation with the United States Ambassador early this morning. The French Prime Minister and Foreign Minister have come over to London at short notice at the invitation of Her Majesty's Government to deliberate with us on these events.

I must tell the House that very grave issues are at stake, and unless hostilities can quickly be stopped, free passage through the Canal will be jeopardised. Moreover, any fighting on the banks of the Canal would endanger the ships actually on passage. The number of crews and passengers involved totals many hundreds, and the value of the ships which are likely to be on passage is about £50 million, excluding the value of the cargoes. Her Majesty's Government and the French Government have accordingly agreed that everything possible should be done to bring hostilities to an end as soon as possible. Their representatives in New York have therefore been instructed to join the United States representative in seeking an immediate meeting of the Security Council. This began at 4.00 p.m.

In the meantime, as a result of the consultations held in London today, the United Kingdom and French Governments have now addressed urgent communications to the Governments of Egypt and Israel. In these we have called upon both sides to stop all warlike action by land, sea and air forthwith and to withdraw their military forces to a distance of 10 miles from the Canal. Further, in order to separate the belligerents and to guarantee freedom of transit through the Canal by the ships of all nations we have asked the Egyptian Government to agree that Anglo-French forces should move temporarily—I repeat temporarily—into key positions at Port Said, Ismailia and Suez. The Governments of Egypt and Israel have been asked to answer this communication with[in] 12 hours. It has been made clear to them that, if at the expiration of that time one or both have not undertaken to comply with these requirements, British and French forces will intervene in whatever strength may be necessary to secure compliance.

I will continue to keep the House informed of the situation.

APPENDIX VIII

ANGLO-FRENCH ULTIMATUM TO THE GOVERNMENTS OF EGYPT AND ISRAEL, 30 OCTOBER 1956

The Governments of the United Kingdom and France have taken note of the outbreak of hostilities between Israel and Egypt. This event threatens to disrupt the freedom of navigation through the Suez Canal on which the economic life of many nations depends.

The Governments of the United Kingdom and France are resolved to do all in their power to bring about the early cessation of hostilities and to safeguard the free passage of the Canal.

They accordingly request the Government of Israel:

(*a*) to stop all warlike action on land, sea and air forthwith;

(*b*) to withdraw all Israeli military forces to a distance of 10 miles east of the Canal.

A communication has been addressed to the Government of Egypt, requesting them to cease hostilities and to withdraw their forces from the neighbourhood of the Canal, and to accept the temporary occupation by Anglo-French forces of key positions at Port Said, Ismailia and Suez.

The United Kingdom and French Governments request an answer to this communication within 12 hours. If at the expiration of that time one or both Governments have not undertaken to comply with the above requirements, United Kingdom and French forces will intervene in whatever strength may be necessary to secure compliance.

Index